STREET BIKE eXtreme

MIKE SEATE

MBI Publishing Company

Professional stunt riders performed the stunts depicted in this book, and even they shouldn't be doing this because frankly, the stunts are completely insane.

Performing them may earn you a Darwin Award for removing your dumb-ass from the gene pool, but trying this at home will almost certainly result in the

destruction of property, death, dismemberment, and the loss of reproductive organs. In other words, don't do it. Neither MBI Publishing or the author accepts any

responsibility should some idiot cause harm to him or herself or others because he or she was damn fool enough to try to replicate any of these stunts. In the

name of everything that is right and holy, do not send us photos or videos of yourself performing stunts. Any such material will be returned unviewed.

First published in 2002 by MBI Publishing Company, Galtier Plaza, Suite 200, 380 Jackson Street, St. Paul, MN 55101-3885 USA

MBI Publishing Company books are also available at discounts in bulk quantity for industrial or sales-promotional use. For details write to Special Sales Manager at Motorbooks International Wholesalers & Distributors, Galtier Plaza, Suite 200, 380 Jackson Street, St. Paul, MN 55101-3885 USA

Library of Congress Cataloging-in-Publication Data available

ISBN: 0-7603-1299-0

Author Bio: Mike Seate is a columnist for the *Pittsburgh Tribune-Review*, a daily newspaper in Pittsburgh, Pennsylvania. He covers urban affairs, the local political scene, emerging pop culture trends, and, of course, motorcycling. Mike has written several motorcycling books and articles that have appeared in *Long Riders, Iron Works, Motorcycle Street & Strip,* and *Cycle World* magazines, among others. An avid rider, Mike does not do stunts. Instead, he opts to use his front wheel to actually steer his motorcycle.

On the front cover: Rob Marley, son of late reggae giant Bob Marley, can ride in this mesmerizing position for miles. *Joe C. Appel*

On the frontispiece: Balance point achieved, now it's time to smile at the crowd as you fly on by. Here, Starboy and *Superbike Magazine* writer "Big" Dave Sonsky executes a wicked handlebar wheelie. *Joe C. Appel*

On the title page: The road to enlightenment is strewn with broken bones. Here, Rev. Paul Sinclair, of London, forgets why professional stunt rider Gary Rothwell insisted that he hold on tight during a wheelie launch. *Camerasport*

On the back cover: *(top)* Team X-Treem's Derrick "D-Mann" Daigle, shown here dressed for success and ready for the possibility of a high-speed dismount. *Joe C. Appel* **(small)** Pauly Sherer, member of the Las Vegas Extremes, demonstrates the Leap of Faith. Any questions? *LVX Photography*

Photos, unless otherwise indicated: Introduction, Chapters 2,3,4: *Joe C. Appel* Chapter 1: *Emap Automotive Ltd*

Edited by Darwin Holmstrom and Chad Caruthers
Layout by Katie Sonmor

Printed in Hong Kong

Contents

Acknowledgments

To bring to life and create a book about a sport that has provided me with years of excitement, thrills, and friendship is a task that definitely falls into the pleasure, not business, category. Regardless of where I've traveled to interview, photograph, or just kick-it with street extreme riders, they've always proven themselves to be the most generous, helpful, and funniest group of motorcyclists I've known in my lifetime of two-wheeling.

Many thanks and endless props to all of the extreme riders I have encountered, and specifically to the following people, for without their help this book would have never reached fruition: Joe Appel; Darwin Holmstrom; Scott, Kevin, Joe, Big Dave; Jesse James; Jan Branaghan at Emap and *Classic Bike Magazine;* J. T. Holt; Adam Chumita; D-Mann; Todd Colbert; Docy Andrews; Cy J. Cyr; Brian J. Nelson; Guinness Stout; Gary Rankin at Whiskey Dick's; Paul Sinclair; Minette Seate at WQED-TV; Ron Christmas at Tucker-Rocky (Blowout 2000!); Mark Hoyer and *Cycle World* magazine; Peter Jones at *Motorcycle Street and Strip*; and Kim Love for having the patience to watch 250 consecutive stunt videos and still act interested.

Mike Seate

Chip McPheeters of Chicago's Loose Cannons on their Four-Way Christ. "The hardest part is making sure everybody makes it up and holds the position at the same time."

Introduction

The first time I saw a motorcycle blast by balanced only on its front wheel, I honestly remember thinking the rider must be in the throes of some horrible accident. In hindsight, I was more right than I could have ever imagined. What I saw on the Akron, Ohio, expressway that summer afternoon five years ago was a "stoppie," as it has come to be known, and like all street extreme tactics, it is an exercise in controlled chaos.

A stoppie, like all street extreme tactics, is an exercise in controlled chaos.

Like all expert athletes practicing their craft, street extreme riders make the impossible look easy. But the road-rash scars on the riders' bodies and the constant sight of busted fairings and scraped exhaust canisters reveal a secret: Even the best-planned wheelies can tip past that delicate balance point and over backward; any tire-chugging burnout can suddenly catch traction and throw both rider and machine to the pavement in the blink of an eye.

Over the course of the couple of years it took to compile the images and conduct the interviews that comprise this book, it became obvious that the inherent danger of street extreme is what makes it so damn cool! For riders, it's the chance to cheat what, to the uninitiated, looks like certain disaster. Crank the throttle, jam on the front stoppers, and every man's a star! This instant "look-at-me" element, coupled with a cool, cavalier attitude toward personal ruin, is a big part of what attracts riders and fans to this wild, cutting-edge sport.

The Starting Line

The factors that gave birth to street extreme boil down to these: Both the bikes and the boys are to blame.

Since the 1930s, a few hearty souls have managed to wring some pretty incredible stunts out of ordinary streetbikes. But without the advent of today's high-horsepower sportbikes—machines that have the most impressive power-to-weight ratios this side of an F-18 fighter jet—and brake and suspension systems far beyond those found on factory-race machines of a

Right: Starboyz' member Kevin Marino makes the most of aerodynamics as he shoots down the quarter-mile.

"Sit tight—I'll drive." The Starboyz make the most of their performance at the AMA Superbike races.

decade before, none of today's street stunts would be possible. Imagine the amount of stress a motorcycle must withstand to land its front wheel on the tarmac from a standstill at over 100 miles per hour. An afternoon of street extreme riding subjects fork seals, wheel bearings, and chassis to impact levels no motorcycle manufacturer in his right mind would even imagine. Prior to street extreme, only highly trained military riders and eccentric professionals would attempt such things and test the boundaries of a bike's structural integrity.

Year after year, though, riders watched excitedly as even the most entry-level sportbikes became tougher and more durable. Todd Colbert, for instance, a 6-foot, 230-pound stunt rider from Florida's Team X-Treem, landed over 1,000 stoppies on his Suzuki GSX-R1100 before

noticing any damage to the rear shock absorber. Try that on a 1969 Norton Commando!

Add to this unchecked horsepower, the constant technology war within the motorcycle industry, and the popularity of extreme sports from skateboarding to freestyle motocross, and you have streetbike extreme. It's no surprise that nearly all of street extreme's hottest young stars have backgrounds in other gravity-defying sports, be it bungee jumping, BMX, riding dirt bikes, or another. The move to street motorcycles, they'll tell you, was simply a matter of looking for bigger, badder thrills.

It's no surprise that nearly all of street extreme's hottest young stars have backgrounds in other gravity-defying sports.

Above and below: *Emap Automotive Ltd.*

Despite the exponential growth in recent years, extreme sports have not traveled an easy road. The marketing of Tony Hawk action figures and Matt Hoffman video games may obscure the fact that only a few years ago skateboarding and BMX biking were illegal in many of the places they were born: streets, backyards, and parking lots. Today, street extreme motorcycling still occupies a place in popular culture just this side of stoplight drag racing. Most everyone involved in the sport has some interesting stories to tell about run-ins with the law or outright-hostile reactions from the public.

Emap Automotive Ltd.

Most everyone involved in the sport has some interesting stories to tell about run-ins with the law or outright-hostile reactions from the public.

Although no American streetbike magazine would dare risk offending its advertisers by running articles about street extreme, and you may not see Ohio's fur-clad Starboyz gracing the cover of a Wheaties box anytime soon, the changing face of sports is slowly, grudgingly, bringing street extreme motorcycling out of the margins and into the mainstream. The last couple of years have seen increased corporate sponsorship, lucrative video distribution deals, an explosion of coverage in the European motorcycling press, and even exposure on U.S. cable television. Streetbike extreme riders, many of whom prefer to compete in the unofficial uniform of baggy jeans, Vans sneakers, and T-shirts (with the occasional helmet worn for the really fast stuff), are increasingly being offered helmet sponsorships and free leathers from industry heavyweights.

In writing this book, we were fortunate to catch some of the sport's longest-running practitioners while they enjoyed their craft out on the double-yellow lines of the streets, where speed, skill, and in-your-face defiance make for one of two-wheeling's most exciting spectacles.

We found a new generation of riders unconcerned with the motorcycle's traditional role as cheap transportation, a generation that rides only for the thrill of the next stunt and nothing more. Linked by the twin demons of instant media gratification and video games, street extreme riders are true products of today's technological age. They are the world's first rebels with a byte.

Though street extreme is best known through its videos, these riders are not the first to film themselves in action for the benefit of their

Handlebar-seated stoppies, as shown by Starboy Scott Caraboolad, are a dangerous and sometimes deadly trick. "When you're up over the bars, you can't steer at all. If anything goes wrong, you're screwed."

peers. Motorcycle enthusiasts have been sharing home movies of themselves enjoying a day in the wind since the 1940s—back when affordable Super 8 cameras flooded the home photography market. This process was repeated in the late 1990s when cheap, hand-held video cameras meant that stunt teams such as The Zoo Crew, Loose Cannons, and Florida's Team X-Treem and others could take video recording their tricks and stunts to new levels. Any rider with an eye for production, a wicked throttle hand, and plenty of cojones could distribute a passable, high-quality stunt video to like-minded riders and enthusiasts across the world in a matter of days.

Street extreme tends to divide motorcyclists into two opposing camps: Those who think videotaping your wheelies is cool, and those who feel the practice gives the sport a bad name.

Of course, for every fan of street extreme, there's at least one detractor. Few popular motorcycle movements, with the exception of maybe the outlaw choppers of the 1960s, have caused such a division within the motorcycle community. Street extreme tends to divide motorcyclists into two opposing camps: Those who think videotaping your wheelies is cool, and those who feel the practice gives the sport a bad name. For proof, just watch the very mixed and always emotional crowd reactions that emerge whenever a Starboyz tape is in the VCR. Nevertheless, the homemade stunt video has proven street extreme's greatest asset. From humble beginnings dubbing tapes in their parents' basements, the Starboyz have, to date, sold over 150,000 copies of their *FTP* videocassettes.

"We were just doing this for fun. We never thought people would buy our tapes. But the next thing we know people are making copies and bike shops are asking us for copies to sell," said Starboy Kevin Marino.

And they're not alone.

Street extreme has helped create an interest in motorcycling among a younger generation of hip, urban riders.

California's Impact Video, started in 1995, has become the country's clearinghouse for amateur street extreme videos, cranking out new titles as fast as riders can make them. Though the figures are not exact, Impact founder Docy Andrews said that about a quarter-million tapes have passed through Impact's distribution center in the past three years alone. When you consider the number of second- and third-generation dubs and pirated foreign versions out there, it's inevitable that street extreme will one day take its place in the motorsports lexicon. In some ways, it already has.

To combat the sport's consistently negative image among law enforcement and motorcycle advocacy groups such as the American Motorcyclist Association (AMA), a group of stunt riders and roadrace promoters formed the Extreme Sportbike Association (XSBA) in 2001. That year, the XSBA staged the first sanctioned street extreme festival at Pocono International Raceway, complete with prize money and television coverage. Formerly a denizen of the passing lane and the police chase, stunt rider Todd Colbert found himself performing at AMA road races throughout the United States, just as professional stunt riders such as Gary Rothwell and Kevin Carmicheal have done at European venues for more than a decade.

Even as the big money and widespread acceptance of drag strip halftime shows and worldwide exposure beckon, many amateur streetbike stunt riders remain satisfied just keepin' it real. They're happier hoistin' a few stand-ups with the fellas on an abandoned industrial park access road than trying to gain acceptance from the fans at a superbike race. You'll never hear the big four manufacturers admit it, but street extreme, for all of its bad-boy imagery and devil-may-care attitudes, has helped create an interest in motorcycling among a younger generation of hip, urban riders. That's something million dollar roadracing teams, fancy sales brochures, and pure technological wizardry could not achieve.

Crank 'em higher, boyz!

Holy smokes! From atop the gas tank, Jon Jon Buccheri of New York's Wheelie Boyz lights up his rear Dunlop.

Chapter 1

Bustin' Out

A Brief History of Stunt Riding

History records the first Wall Of Death motorcycle stunt shows—where riders whip tiny board-track race bikes around a wooden drum, held aloft by sheer centrifugal force—as having appeared at carnivals and county fairs as early as 1913. This was back when such motorcycles as Indian's 45ci, side-valve V-Twins operated what old-timers call total-loss oil systems, which literally dumped the used lube onto the pavement. Try to pull an endo on one of these!

To raise morale and fighting spirit (read: bring us more cannon fodder) during both world wars, military motorcycle corps commanders began organizing their well-trained riders to stage shows for new recruits. With an impressionable public looking on, such teams as Britain's White Helmets of the Royal Signal Corps started to show off slow-motion moves including the multiple-rider moving pyramid as early as 1927. Subjected to an intense, five-month training period, the White Helmets (later parodied by the Purple Helmets, a scooter-riding "stunt" team operating under the motto, "We Suck") could climb ladders mounted to the frames of their Triumph Bonnevilles and Speed Twins, steer with their feet on the handlebars, and carry up to 12 men on a single bike.

To survive as a biker while ducking bullets and whipping around land mines takes some serious ability, and military bike riders often came home from the service with some of the maddest streetbike skills around. As seen in the independently released film, *Those Were the Days,* a contingent of World War II veterans riding Harleys and Indians can be seen doing seat-stands, circular burnouts, and other stunts you wouldn't believe possible on 600-pound motorcycles with rigid rear suspensions and drum brakes!

Street extreme riding has been a **part of the American biker scene** for about as long as anyone can remember.

In fact, though the AMA and mainstream motorcycle magazines would be loath to admit it, street extreme riding has been a part of the American biker scene for about as long as anyone can remember. The fabled Hollister, California, motorcycle-rally-turned-riot, a July 1947 event that spawned the outlaw biker culture and served as inspiration for the 1954 biker movie classic *The Wild One,* made headlines after groups of beered-up veterans staged what newspaper reports tabbed "an illegal speed and stunt exhibition" along Hollister's main drag. In a famous press picture released at the time, a rider is being lectured by a Hollister policeman while a curious crowd looks on—a scene that any of today's street stunt riders can surely relate to.

Old-timers will tell you that in those restless days, drinking hard and riding hard were the twin marks of whether you were a real biker. Because lots of 1950s bikers were broke, adventurous types, they spent a lot of time on their two-wheelers, where they developed a deep familiarity with

Helmetless and riding in neckties and dress shirts, England's Cytrix Display Team epitomizes Britain's gentlemanly biking spirit as it toured motorcycle gatherings on their Matchless single, circa 1955.

the dynamics and physical limits of their machines, much as they had during wartime.

During the next 20 years, amateur street stunt riding was mostly forgotten. A new generation of smaller, lighter Japanese streetbikes didn't really have the horsepower for one-wheeled antics and stoplight-to-stoplight drag racing. With the chopper craze in full swing by the mid-1960s, most domestic bikes had been modified to the point where they were only likely to lift a front wheel when being hoisted into the back of a tow truck.

As always, there were exceptions. The 1982 documentary film *Hell's Angels Forever* features several scenes where longhaired hell-raisers are shown popping wheelies on stretch choppers, with one even managing a wicked seat-stand at highway speed. But for the most part, stunt riding was limited to professional stuntmen, such as the self-proclaimed Wheelie King, Doug Domokos.

Doug Domokos

Domokos burst onto the scene in the mid-1970s, a bell-bottom-wearing, joke-cracking young rider who had taken his skills as a street stunt rider to major success. Domokos was a practitioner of slow, nearly vertical wheelies that were as much a display of sheer balls as they were of perfect balance. Street extreme riders would be amazed to know that Domokos' self-promotion skills and streetbike talents actually helped him land a paid sponsorship from Kawasaki Motors in the early 1980s, an endorsement virtually unheard of in today's conservative corporate climate. He soon thereafter started showing up at events on a huge green Kawasaki KZ 1300, a six-cylinder behemoth that weighed nearly 700 pounds. Though Domokos was professional enough to woo mainstream media coverage from ABC's *Wide World of Sports* and command five-figure salaries for his shows, he was still something of a bad boy: In the early 1980s, he almost lost his corporate backing when, egged on by the crowd at a Supercross race, he launched the KZ 1300 up, onto, and then over some poor spectator's rental car, flattening its roof in the process.

Not many riders would have an easy time trying to outrun these West Berlin motorcycle cops, who appeared at the Annual West German Police Sports Gala in 1968. Their police-issue BMW is outfitted with an elaborate steel framework that rotates during the ride.

Domokos, due in part to his unique cheerfulness and charisma, took hooligan stunt riding to places it still has not returned. In his popular 1980 book *Wheelyin' With The King,* Domokos comes off as a self-help guru who just happens to believe personal enlightenment comes from riding a motorcycle on one wheel. Willing to do anything for attention and applause, he would wheelie dirt bikes through burning walls, over ramps, and once soaked his jeans in gasoline and set himself on fire before riding his bike into a nearby lake.

Domokos was a practitioner of slow, near vertical wheelies that were as much a display of sheer balls as they were of perfect balance.

Over a 20-year career, Domokos appeared on network television numerous times and amassed several Guinness World Records. Working as his own mechanic, he rigged up a tiny electric motor that kept his front wheel rotating while he pulled cross-county wheelies. This created a gyroscopic effect that helped Domokos when he convinced city officials to allow him to ride a wheelie through Lombard Street in San Francisco, the hilly city's longest, twistiest boulevard. In 1984, he convinced sponsors and television news crews to follow him as he promised to—and eventually did—ride a single, continuous wheelie for 145 miles across the desert Southwest.

Never one to rest easy, Domokos later topped that record by adding some 150 additional miles.

Evel Knievel

To call 1950s Butte, Montana, boring would be like calling *The Lawrence Welk Show* a little old-fashioned. Locals remember the mining and cattle-distribution town as a place where recreation was limited to "getting drunk, or getting drunk and driving fast."

Those were the entertainment options facing Robert Craig "Bobby" Knievel as he grew up in the dusty cow town during the Eisenhower era. Bobby was a typical spirited kid who had his share of run-ins with the authorities, mostly for pulling pranks and impressing the locals with his displays of motorcycling skills. Bobby Knievel, whom townspeople nicknamed "Evel" due to his reputation for mischief and fearlessness on a two-wheeler, was eventu-

The all-time king of motorcycle stunt riders, Bobby "Evel" Knievel botches a landing at London's Wembly Arena in May 1975. This crash that totaled yet another Harley-Davidson XR750 was but one of the increasingly difficult long-distance jumps that catapulted Knievel to fame, fortune, and hospital emergency rooms throughout his 20-year career.

ally barred from riding along Butte's Main Street, where the local hot rodders and bikers gathered.

He was arrested and jailed more times than he can rightly remember for doing many of the same stunts that street extreme riders perform today. That Knievel could hoist block-long wheelies and ride his 1950s-era Brit bikes down flights of steps (and on more than one occasion, through crowded bars) was testament to how tough he really was. "He used a motorcycle that most people wouldn't try and jump over curbs with to jump busses," was how England's *Bike Magazine* summed up Knievel's legendary courage.

Of course, Knievel was not the first rider to gain notoriety and mad dollars for riding wicked.

But Knievel, a hard-gambling, Jack Daniel's–swillin' Montana bad boy, is considered by many to be the father of both street extreme and freestyle motocross, mainly because he took his improvised act from the streets to the big time, clocking millions in the faces of his many detractors. Knievel embodied the bullheaded man's-man thinking that characterizes street extreme to this day. He rode an overweight, underpowered Harley-Davidson XR 750 flat-track racer for incredible (and, some say incredibly stupid) jumps over lines of buses and semi-trailers at a time when imported dirt bikes would have made his career, and doctors, much easier to get along with. That Knievel suffered more funky breaks than a Wu Tang album—he often chose to deaden the pain from his more than 30 bone fractures with whiskey and all-night gambling binges at Las Vegas casinos—only adds to his stature as a street extreme visionary.

> That Knievel could hoist **block-long wheelies** and ride his 1950s-era Brit bikes down flights of steps was testament to how tough he really was.

Long before Nike coined the phrase, Knievel was a just do it sort of athlete. In a 2000 interview with *Big Bikes* magazine, he explained that during 20 years of stunt riding on and off the streets, he never developed a technique or system for popping wheelies. "It's just something you can either do or you can't. You need incredible balance to hold a wheelie just right," he said. Knievel, who once bragged about having made $60 million through endorsements, a popular line of toys, and stunt shows, only to lose $61 million gambling and chasing women, learned his craft through plain-old street riding.

Like most of today's street extreme experts, Knievel was something of an all-around athlete and thrill-seeker from childhood. He had tried his hand at rodeo riding and became a fairly competent ski jumper by his late teens. After a stint as a truck driver in the U.S. Army in the late 1950s, Knievel sought more excitement and started racing motorcycles in dirt-track events throughout the Southwest. At one event, he saw how fervently the crowd reacted to an automobile stunt show by the legendary Joey Chitwood and decided then and there to launch his own two-wheeled version. The show was initially some 2 1/2 hours long, with a small jump—the early vaults were over low-concept obstacles including a box of rattlesnakes—included as a grand finale.

Of course the showman in Knievel realized that with more elaborate motorcycle jumps there was big money to be made and big-time media attention awaiting. By 1967, Knievel was one of the country's biggest-drawing stars and the world's best-known daredevil. The next year, an attempt to loft his Triumph 650 Bonneville some 50 yards across the fountain at Caesar's Palace in Las Vegas ended with Knievel in a month-long coma and a solid place in the motorcycle history books.

"I started with Norton, switched to Triumph, and eventually ended up doing my jumps on Harleys. The Harley-Davidsons had way too much torque and they'd end up flexing sideways up in the air and that screwed up some of my landings," Knievel said in a recent interview. The improvements in motorcycle suspension and technology that Knievel really needed were 20 years away. But when the industry started cutting loose with stiffer front forks, rugged mono-shock suspension systems, and, most important, rev-happy motors that could hoist a front wheel or spin a back tire in less time than it took Knievel to kick-start his old Hog, street extreme was on its way.

Knievel, **a hard-gambling, Jack Daniel's-swillin' bad boy,** *is considered by many to be the father of both street extreme and freestyle motocross.*

Following in the footsteps of Evel Knievel, Britain's Eddie Kidd successfully vaults 16 double-decker buses in this 1978 motorcycle jump.

Gary Rothwell

Gary Rothwell was a Welsh lad whose motorcycle endeavors were inspired by none other than Artie Nyquist. Dutch rider Nyquist, a goofy showman who wowed spectators at European Grand Prix races by skiing behind his KZ 1300 wearing traditional Dutch wooden shoes, was among the first to exploit the tremendous power delivery of a big-inch Japanese sportbike. Dressed in a very Michael Jackson–esque drum major's uniform, Nyquist inspired a generation of young, would-be European stunt riders, including Rothwell.

Like Nyquist and Domokos, Rothwell taught himself to perform stunts on the streets, astride one of Kawasaki's unwieldy KZ 1300s. Though the bike appeared more suited to pulling backyard stumps than defying gravity, Rothwell managed to perfect a lengthy routine on the big bike, originating and popularizing many of the signature moves of street extreme.

Rothwell taught himself to perform stunts on the streets, astride one of Kawasaki's unwieldy KZ 1300s.

Brian J. Nelson Photography

The stoppie and 180 endo, the handlebar-seated wheelie, the elaborate practice of writing one's initials in burned rubber—these are all attributed to Rothwell, who performed his moves for startled and delighted crowds at British bike meets and pub parking lots for most of the early 1990s. Almost by accident, a fresh-from-the-pub 19-year-old Rothwell decided to show his stuff to the crowds gathered at the annual Isle of Man TT roadraces. A friend caught his curbside stunt show—and Rothwell's subsequent arrest by Isle of Man police—on video, and *Performance Bike* magazine photographers ran a feature on Rothwell, calling him, "a genius on a motorcycle." The video clips made it onto his *Showtime* video, one of the first and best-selling motorcycle stunt videos ever made. By the time *Showtime* had been released, in 1995, Rothwell and his wife, Joan, had perfected *Wonder Wheels,* a traveling stunt show that made headlines across Europe, Great Britain, and, due to the overwhelming response of the *Showtime* video, in the United States.

Steel-soled riding boots help to make skiing behind a fast-moving stuntbike possible. Atop a 130-horsepower Suzuki GSX-R1100, Gary Rothwell learned to ski at speeds up to 155 miles per hour!
Brian J. Nelson Photography

Behind the wicked, high-speed stunts and death-defying La-Z-Boys at 140 miles per hour, the most famous face in stunt riding is your basic friendly bloke next door. The easygoing Rothwell admits to practicing very little, unless he's preparing to break a new record or two. "I generally just mess about for a few minutes before each show," he admitted sheepishly.

From his earliest appearances at British superbike races, Rothwell has always run a highly professional show. He no longer performs his moves on the street, for instance, and always appears in full race leathers wearing a full-face helmet. Working with a team of professional technicians, Rothwell often runs his immaculately prepared streetfighter Suzuki GSX-R1100 to prerecorded music or in televised attempts to break world records.

Like Domokos, Rothwell has claimed quite a few records in his day, including several for skiing behind his motorcycle (most recently at 170 miles per hour) and another for hoisting a wheelie with 14 people on board.

The easygoing Rothwell admits to practicing very little, unless he's preparing to break a new record or two.

"I never expected this to take off the way it did. I mean I always had mates who could ride well, pull a wheelie or two on a dirt bike, but for people to get so excited about stunt riding, that really took me by surprise. When *Performance Bike* shot the first pictures of me, a lot of people thought I was a bit daft and that I'd probably kill myself," Rothwell said.

Rothwell, who has only suffered a broken ankle in nearly a decade of performing, set the standard for European stunt riders, who, in 1997, had become large enough in number to launch the first European Stunt Riding Championships. Just as with street extreme in the United States, you'll get as many variations on why the Euro stunt scene took off and who started it as you will variations of the wheelie. But the general consensus is that Rothwell

There are no ladders or props for acrobatics, but this two-up wheelie shows the influence that early stunt riding had on Gary Rothwell and others.

Another stunt that was made possible by the vast progress in motorcycle brake and tire design during the past 10 years was the two-up stoppie.

Photos pages 24 and 25: Brian J. Nelson Photography

Where U.S. street extreme riders often cover their stunt bikes in fake fur to deflect crash damage, Gary Rothwell, like many British riders, prefers the naked Streetfighter bikes. The Streetfighters originally derived from numerous crashed sportbikes' owners, who grew tired of replacing dinged fairings. *Brian J. Nelson Photography*

Gary Rothwell has claimed and reclaimed the Guinness World Record for "Most Persons on a Wheelie." Here, he loads up his Suzuki Bandit with three extra riders for a high-speed pass at Brainerd International Raceway in Minnesota. *Brian J. Nelson Photography*

was behind the movement's rapid growth.

"People will try and deny it, but all of our lads— (1997 European Stunt Riding champ) Kevin Carmicheal, Dave Coates, and everybody else—started riding on the streets. That's the only place where a young lad can learn how to do these crazy, potentially dangerous things. Nobody's going to give you a drag strip or an abandoned airport runway when you're 19 and [broke] and want to practice your wheelies," said Robbie Allan, one of Scotland's better-known stunt-show promoters.

Up–and– Coming Stunt Riders

Allan, of Boghead, Warshickshire's M&R Promotions, staged many of the United Kingdom's inaugural stunt contests, shepherding such unknown competitors as Dave Coates, Craig Jones, Sonnie Ferguson, and Jimmy Fireblade from street riders to international stars. The annual European Stunt Riding Championship has been captured for fans each year by Duke Video, the United Kingdom's leading stunt video distributor, and Allan stays busy booking riders into a wide variety

The release of the *Showtime* video by British stuntman ace Gary Rothwell helped launch a worldwide stuntbike revolution. *G.R. Productions*

of venues, from custom-bike shows to a series of drag races sponsored by the very stunt-friendly *Streetfighters* magazine.

Regardless, though, of how well these highly skilled riders honed their talents on the rainy streets of England, Allan is quick to point out that, "What your American lads do is far, far different from what you see over here. "It's compulsory that they perform within certain parameters for distance and height for wheelies and stoppies, for instance."

This has not put a damper on the competition, Allan said, with new riders springing up to challenge the established order practically every week. In 1998, a 33-year-old Brazilian mountain-bike rider, Antonio Carlos "A. C." Farias, burst onto the European scene and practically rewrote the rulebook of stunt riding and physical dexterity.

Antonio Carlos "A. C." Farias burst onto the European scene and practically rewrote the rulebook of stunt riding and physical dexterity.

Farias, Allan remembers, practiced his jack-crazy one-sided vertical wheelies and nonhands stunts on his Honda CBR600 by riding a mountain bike for several hours without the front wheel. His butter-smooth moves and uncanny ability to virtually spin his CBR in a tiny, circular wheelie for what seems an eternity caused many competitors to run back to the practice strips in a panic, Allan said. "He can do his routine in half the space of the other guys and on a tiny little 600. By the next year, you had guys like Dave Coates riding backwards with another rider perched on his shoulders, Scotsman Magnus Carrlson skiing two-up, and Kevin Carmicheal going so far as to remove the front wheel from his Honda CBR900, launching his wheelies from a set of axle chocks."

Allan has reason to be enthusiastic about the future of street stunt riding in Europe after seeing a new Scottish rider, Dave Taylor, navigate the entire 38-mile Isle of Man TT course—blind corners, sheer mountain cliffs and all—on one wheel. "One day I'd love to see what some of our guys could do against the American street riders. That would be a great show," he said.

Chapter 2

The Starboyz
Climb On and Watch the Fur Fly!

In 1993, Kevin Marino, of Akron, Ohio, had a reputation as one of the area's better streetbike riders. Marino, then in his early 20s, could whip his Honda CBR600 around a tight corner fast enough to have groups of slower riders following him on weekends to learn his style. Like thousands of other talented young riders, Marino started riding dirt bikes with his family at an age when most boys were still struggling to master T-ball.

As a result, he'd learned to pull an impressive wheelie on his little 50-cc Honda—when his Mom wasn't looking, that is—a skill that proved even more satisfying when he took it to the streets on a big bike about 10 years later.

"People ask me how I learned to do wheelies, but it's just something I've been doing since I started riding. You get to the point where you just get a feel for what gear you have to be in to lift the front end and after that, it just goes," he said.

With both the Mid-Ohio Sportscar Course and the amateur racer's haven, the Nelsen Ledges roadrace track, both only a short ride from his Akron home, Marino eventually found himself drawn to the idea of putting his skills to test on a track. That summer, he enrolled in one of Fastraxx racing's advanced street rider courses, a training ground for future roadracers. "I'd always wanted to get into roadracing, but once I got into it, I realized it's too expensive and there's just too many rules. It seems like there's always somebody telling you what you can and can't do," he recalled.

Nevertheless, one day while howling down Nelsen's back straightaway, Marino passed Nelsen Ledges' tiny spectator grandstands. The temptation was too much to resist, and he popped the clutch on his F2, which sent the front wheel clawing skyward. The track officials were not impressed and told Marino as much.

"They started yelling at me about how stupid and dangerous wheelies are on a track and I thought, 'Screw this, I'm outty,'" Marino said. That was the last time he or any other member of the Starboyz rode in a sanctioned, organized competition.

Legs over the bars, (left to right) Scott Caraboolad, "Big Dave" Sonsky, and Kevin Marino strike a pose familiar for Ohio motorists—and law enforcement.

"Screw this, I'm outty," Marino thought. That was the last time he or any other member of the Starboyz rode in a sanctioned, organized competition.

There are people who follow orders and people who have to do things their own way, and the Starboyz are certainly listed in the latter category. After Marino's brief venture into roadracing, he went right back to the streets where he continued hoisting an ever-impressive display of one-wheel moves for a growing following of local sportbike riders. Though original Starboyz members Kevin Marino, Scott

Kevin Marino's flying wheelie is reminiscent of the horizontal launches favored by early Bonneville Salt Flats racers. Shirts are optional.

Caraboolad, and Joe Frazier can't recall precisely when or where the three came together, they're sure their meeting was inevitable, because they all shared the same idea of what riding a motorcycle was all about.

"Yeah, I think it's cool to be able to whip around corners and do knee-downs like those European cats do, but when it comes to riding wheelies and doing stunts, that's the real fun. I mean, how many people do you meet who can actually do stunts and do them well without hurting themselves or anybody else?" Caraboolad said.

In time, he'd find out the answer to that question.

The Birth of the Starboyz

A loosely connected group of sportbike riders routinely gathered for high-speed runs along Interstate 76, which winds its way around the city center of Akron and often carries a haze, the result of numerous nearby industrial plants. Passing through modest neighborhoods and abandoned tire factories, the busy highway stays filled on most weekdays with thousands of commuters and impatient truckers.

With traffic speeds varying between a 55-mile-per-hour crawl and up to 90, it's a dangerous stretch of mostly elevated highway. To a stunt rider, Route 76 was something else entirely: the best makeshift arena in the world.

Night after night for most of 1994, Marino, Frazier, and Caraboolad would ride with 20 to 30 other sportbikers up and down the interstate, cranking wheelies and, in Frazier's words, "scaring the living dog shit" out of motorists who never expected to see a motorcycle blaze past their window on one wheel at 100 miles per hour.

Professional stuntman Gary Rothwell tags a track with a display of circular burnouts. Leave your mark and they'll never forget you. Rothwell has been known to write the initials of audience members on the pavement with his smoking rear Dunlop.

> ## The Starboyz are simply seeking thrills and a healthy side order of fame, and not much else.

"We were doing this just about every night for a whole summer and we realized that the three of us were getting better and better at it. There were other guys, too, but the three of us really hit it off," Frazier said. It would figure. Marino, Caraboolad, and Frazier are all about the same age, and all three had wanted to meet other guys willing to push the envelope on the street. "We never thought back then, 'Let's start a professional stunt team and make a lot of money.' We were just doing this to see who was the best," Caraboolad said.

Critics have accused stunt riders of harboring some great existential angst or an underlying obsession with death, but when the guys are gearing up for an afternoon of highway runs, the vernacular seldom gets that deep. The Starboyz are simply seeking thrills and a healthy side order of fame, and not much else.

Just a few weeks ago, this CBR Honda was a pristine, show room–condition motorcycle. Now, Scott Caraboolad busts a vertical stoppie with the help of copious amounts of duct tape and zipties. Note the lack of tread on the front tire.

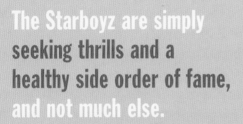

Left: Here's a variation of the gas-tank wheelie, but this time Scott Caraboolad clicks his heels in a motocross-style cancan variation.

Be honest: Does this stoppie make my butt look big?

The flamingo wheelie by the always-photogenic "Big Dave" Sonsky. If only we could say the same for his bike.

THE NEW GENERATION

The Starboyz can count themselves among a new generation of bikers for whom simply riding a motorcycle is not enough, even with the inherent dangers and heart-in-the-throat excitement of biking. They belong to a growing contingent of riders who want serious thrills, all the time.

"It gets boring as hell just riding around all day," Marino said. "I mean, I see these old dudes who travel all over the county on their Gold Wings, and I give them props for keeping at it, but unless I'm cranking a wheelie or somebody's watching me, I just don't get off on riding."

This is the same motivation that drives surfers to shoot waves during tropical storms and skydivers who up the ante by performing midair acrobatics or jumping in elaborate formations.

It's this same need to constantly reinvent a sport and lend it new excitement that has motivated the Starboyz and other stunt teams from the start. Frazier remembers simply meeting on early Sunday mornings, when there was hardly any traffic, and they would embark on long, unorganized practice runs to see who could hold a stand-up wheelie the longest without falling or getting caught by the cops. Whoever came away with the biggest display of skills and sheer balls won some sort of unspoken bragging rights—that and the admiration of his fellow riders.

Joe Frazier and "Big Dave" Sonsky unload the bikes for a practice session. Too-frequent cop stops caused the Starboyz and other street extreme riders to trailer, rather than ride, their motorcycles to and from performances.

> ## "It gets boring as hell just riding around all day. Unless I'm cranking a wheelie or somebody's watching me, I just don't get off on riding."
> –Kevin Marino, Starboyz

Soon, though, people started getting up early to catch the show, Frazier said. Over the length of that summer, crowds of street drag racers in their Miatas and Spyders started gathering on highway overpasses to watch the nightly wheelie procession. With their growing popularity, the bikers started to notice increasing police presence. When the blue-and-reds flashed in the rear rider's rearview mirrors, there was an unspoken rule to just *go for it,* Marino remembers. "A lot of guys didn't have a license or their paperwork straight, or maybe they just thought it was fun, so we'd always run for it," said Frazier.

It helped, too, that the crew soon realized that many Ohio police departments are required to disengage high-speed chases with motorcycles when the officer in question feels the pursuit could endanger other motorists. Police chases are dangerous and highly illegal—but fun—games of cat and mouse.

Police chases are dangerous and highly illegal—but fun—games of cat and mouse.

As the trio's talent and rapidly advancing stunt skills distanced them from the rest of the local sportbike crowd, they happened on a silly idea. "I thought, with so much attention from the police, we're kind of like stars out here on the highway. I was working in a bike shop at the time and ordered up some of Vanson's Star jackets," Marino said. With matching Vanson leathers on the group's backs, their followers started calling them the Starboyz.

The easily identifiable jackets helped galvanize the crew's image with the droves of other riders in the area who showed up to see what all

The Switchback Extension is a stunt dependent on the rider clearing the handlebars without flaw. One nudge and it's all over. Popular variations include the Switchback Insane, done standing on your head!

the hubbub was about. As testament to how hot the police pressure was during the Starboyz' early days of pulling wheelies in Akron, any sportbike rider wearing a Vanson Star jacket drew squad cars like a doughnut shop draws cops.

For example, during summer 2001, the Starboyz were driving in their SUV to a performance in Miami when an Ohio radio station ran a broadcast about a Starboy getting apprehended for reckless driving on the Ohio Turnpike. In reality, Caraboolad said, "Anybody who rides wheelies now is considered a Starboy, and meanwhile, we don't even ride around Akron anymore."

Nobody can remember the exact number of tickets, crashes, and crosstown chases, but the Starboyz' perpetual legal wrangling over traffic citations quickly became the stuff of local legend. But it wasn't as though that bothered anyone.

"By then we were getting huge crowds on weekends and we'd entered a few wheelie contests (at Thompson Dragway, a Cleveland-area quarter-mile), so people were starting to know who we were," Marino said

Few people who hadn't seen the illegal street shows could imagine that the Starboyz were for real. The only streetbike stunts most riders had seen by then were those on the slick-looking, professionally produced *Showtime* video from British stunt rider Gary Rothwell.

IMITATION IS ART

All three Starboyz and numerous other street extreme riders you meet will attest to the incredible influence Rothwell had on their deciding to ride stunts. "Rothwell, he was the original. When I saw him, I remember thinking, I didn't even know you could do circular donuts on a streetbike. I went outside right after watching that tape and did it myself," said Starboy Frazier.

Though Rothwell preferred the relatively safe environment of the track to the streets, riders without access to closed courses were determined to emulate their hero anyplace they could, from the local Hooters' parking lot to freeways packed tight with minivans and big rigs.

This emulation of the stunts seen on videotapes is part and parcel of how the street extreme movement grows and develops new skills. With no real or established stunt riding how-to tapes available, riders simply buy the latest videos and learn from imitation. Hours spent studying the move in a European Stunt Riding Championships video is how Marino learned to turn around and remount his CBR backward while moving at 75 miles per hour. And the extraordinarily difficult handstands favored by West Coast street extreme expert J. T. Holt were first seen in Las Vegas Extremes' initial video, *Las Vegas Extremes,* released in 1999.

> ### With no real or established stunt riding how-to tapes available, riders simply buy the latest videos and learn from imitation.

All of the crew or riders have developed their own particular trademark stunts, such as Todd Colbert's nearly vertical nac-nac wheelies or Derrick "D-Mann" Daigle's Leap of Faith from the motorcycle's seat to the gas tank. But, like skaters and snowboarders, few riders are protective of, or threatened by, other riders doing their moves. Perhaps a downside of this free exchange of ideas is that Rothwell's maneuvers have inspired a youthful cadre of impostors, many of whom can match him trick for trick and are willing to perform for free or close to it.

However, in Frazier's opinion, sharing ideas helps keep street extreme fresh. "No two people do a stunt exactly alike, so even if you started something, somebody else may shift their weight a different way or end up with different results," he said.

After countless screenings of the *Showtime* videotape, Marino, who had long held a fascination with videotaping, decided to rig up his $400 Sears camcorder to the tank of his motorcycle for a few runs through Akron's notoriously dense rush-hour traffic. "I just thought it would be fun to get it down on tape what kind of wild shit we were doing," he said with a shrug.

FTP Hits the Set

His hair freshly dyed a funky emerald green, Marino and girlfriend (and later wife), Lisa, made for a striking sight as they strolled through the 1997 Cycle World International exposition at Cleveland's IX Center. The former U.S. Army tank assembly factory was filled with the motorcycle industry's flashiest new machines and celebrities, but everywhere Marino went, a curious crowd started to gather.

In the plastic garbage bag he toted around were copies of a homemade videotape featuring 40 minutes of hypersonic thrash music and some of the most unbelievable street-bike footage anyone had ever seen. The quality was grainy and had all the production value of a ransom tape, but the crowd that weekend didn't care. *FTP 1,* as the tape would later come to be known, was clearly the most talked-about attraction at the IX Center.

Marino recalls simply walking up to the various merchandise and accessories booths and asking if he could show a few minutes of a tape that he and some buddies had made. The results were electrifying. "People were just stopping whatever they were doing and screaming 'Holy shit!' I only had about six copies because I'd just made it to show to my friends and trade back and forth, but all of a sudden, these major nationwide retailers were like, 'How many of these can you sell me? They'll go like hot-cakes.'" Motorcyclists may be a disparate community, but riders compose one of the most tightly connected subcultures in the world. Within this intertwined framework, it didn't take long for word to spread about this crazy bunch of boys from Ohio who had taped themselves busting stunts—in broad daylight and out in the streets, no less.

Caraboolad, Frazier, and Marino soon found themselves rushing back and forth between the VCR dub-decks and local bike shops just to keep the curious supplied. The trio swears that the subsequent extreme bike video

FTP 1 (come on, you can guess what that stands for): Forty minutes of hypersonic thrash music and some of the most unbelievable streetbike footage anyone had ever seen.

How many times do you have to pull a full-vertical wheelie before they become second nature? Steady pressure on the rear brake keeps the bike from picking up speed or tipping over backward.

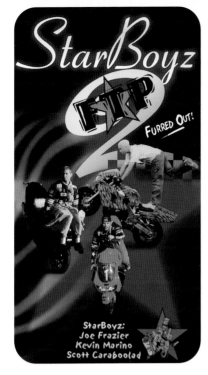

StarBoyz:
Joe Frazier
Kevin Marino
Scott Caraboolad

Shot on location across the United States, the Starboyz' *FTP 2* video was as slick and engrossing as street extreme films get. To date, no wanna-be imitators have been able to re-create the level of madness of this bestseller.

revolution that *FTP 1* set off was unintentional. Original copies were released without any fancy labeling, and cover graphics were added only after the guys realized that there was indeed an audience for this kind of motorcycling mayhem. "I mean, to be honest, I wasn't really sure I wanted my folks and everybody else to know that I was out there doin' all this crazy shit," Frazier confessed.

People stopped by to visit Marino, who sold parts at a Suzuki shop, and asked for copies of *FTP 1* (come on, you can guess what the initials stand for) and calls flowed in from shops and individuals across the country who had somehow heard of the Starboyz' tape. With dozens of street extreme videos now stocking the shelves at bike shops today, it's easy to underestimate the shock value and originality of *FTP 1* when it first surfaced. Most motorcyclists had never seen a stoppie or rolling burnout, let alone a seemingly endless repertoire of them done on public roadways.

The crew, sometimes numbering nearly 20 riders, is shown breaking nearly every law of gravity and traffic in the book. They are seen whipping around slow-moving traffic in some truly butt-clenching street races, performing rolling stoppies on rain-slicked streets, and trying desperately to prove that motorcycling has no limits. The Starboyz even exhibited a sense of humor by running tapes of their stunts (and near misses) backward, and there was even a hilarious bit involving tiny 50-cc pocket bikes on a four-lane freeway at night.

> The crew, sometimes numbering nearly 20 riders, is shown **breaking nearly every law of gravity and traffic in the book.**

Marino has admitted that what he misses most about those innocent early days is how nice his GSX-Rs looked. Today, after years of spring-bashing stunt landings, the Starboyz' mounts are a far cry from the polished and chromed-out machines visible in *FTP 1.*

The Bikes

Journalists have questioned the Starboyz extensively about why they choose to run mostly GSX-R750 Suzukis (Marino) or Honda CBR900s (Frazier, Caraboolad, and occasional freelance stunt riders and moto-journalist "Big Dave" Sonsky), but their choice of machines, it turns out, has less

Roadracing audiences, accustomed to only brief, finish-line wheelies, are exposed to a sidesaddle wheelstand at the Mid-Ohio Sportscar Course. When four-time World Superbike Champion "King" Carl Fogarty saw the Starboyz riding like this on the streets of Daytona in 2000, he invited them to star in his new lifestyle video. "I've won four world titles and I have no idea how those guys do that."

Part-time Starboy Tave Stanley leaving a black streak on the sport of roadracing down Mid-Ohio Sportscar Course's back straightaway. "They made us wear full leathers in the middle of July. It was crazy-hot, but the crowd went nuts."

to do with brand loyalty or stunt abilities than sheer affordability. The bikes in *FTP 1* had to be cheap because several are destroyed on camera, scenes that only added to the reckless flavor of the tape.

Frazier has been Dumpster-diving at motorcycle repair shops for years, recovering well-worn sportbike tires that other customers throw away. "When you're doing burnouts, tires will only last about 15 or 20 minutes into a show. I went through 100 in one month last year so we stopped buying them new and went to old, beat-up ones that don't have to last long."

Joe has been Dumpster diving at motorcycle repair shops for years, recovering well-worn sportbike tires that other customers throw away.

"You can get tons of parts for GSX-Rs and CBRs because they're two of the top-selling sportbikes. And if you watch enough stunt videos you'll notice people are always trying to imitate us, and there's always somebody flipping one. That means you can go to a salvage yard and get stuff dirt cheap," Marino said.

Caraboolad's garage in Akron looks like the set of a biking *Sanford and Son,* with forks, spare wheels, and enough dinged-up used parts littering the floor to easily build a half-dozen Honda CBRs. His current bike, a 1998 model with its trademark stoved-in gas tank from too many handlebar-seated wheelies and an exhaust canister flattened on end from his crawling, first-gear vertical wheelies, cost just $1,300.

Stunt riding is notoriously hard on motorcycles, even bikes as durable as the recent-model sportbikes. Common on street extreme bikes are engine cases that are soldered back together, fairings "secured" with zip-ties, and twisted or bent forks. The Starboyz are frequently asked to perform stunts on their fans' own motorcycles, which Marino said he'll grudgingly do, but he always warns people what to expect.

"If you give me your brand-new, nice, polished-out sportbike and let me stoppie it and slam down wheelies all day, it's just not gonna be the same bike when I get done. I always tell people, 'You have a nice, new bike. Keep it that way.' That's why our bikes are such pieces of shit. You can't stunt a bike and have it stay nice very long," he said.

The multicolored fake fur that started appearing on the Starboyz' bikes in 1998 is said to be held in place because it cushions the plastic motorcycle body parts if (or more likely, when) they smack the pavement. Caraboolad claims this is all a myth, that the fur just helps the team's bikes look more distinctive. Still, from the frequent sightings of bikes throughout *FTP 2* with missing bodywork, it's clear that the fur must have some purpose beyond simple aesthetics.

Common on street extreme bikes are engine cases that are soldered back together, fairings "secured" with zip-ties, and twisted or bent forks.

Lights, Camera, You're Busted!

Trashing bikes, popping wheelies where people least expect it, and generally goofing off on a motorcycle are not only fun for the rider, but people would pay to watch it, the trio soon realized. Stunts and other things that hundreds of times had nearly gotten the Starboyz arrested suddenly had the whole world beating a path to their door. But unfortunately, the media, followed by the police, soon came knocking, too.

As hundreds of copies of *FTP 1* circulated around the Cleveland/Akron area, it was inevitable that one cassette would find its way into the hands of a television news crew. Motorists, already peeved at this now well-known crew of bikers who routinely cut through and around stalled traffic, were a ripe audience for the sensational report aired on a Cleveland Fox TV News affiliate in May 1999.

In a turn straight out of the biker movies of the 1960s, investigative reporter Janice Martin led the broadcast with the headline "killer cycle psychos on the rampage," and filled the next 10 minutes with an odd montage of outraged drivers, cops, and parents. Repeatedly, the film showed a segment of *FTP 1* where Marino's GSX-R passed a slow-moving Cuyahoga County school bus on the right; a fearful voice-over is heard asking, "What if these were your children?" It was just what Akron needed to hype a new menace into creation.

In an odd turn, Fox News interviewed several Harley types from an antihelmet organization. These middle-aged folks, who were themselves once known for pissing off the populace, somehow managed to completely miss the irony in labeling the Starboyz "a menace to society!" Reporter Martin, who defended her piece by asking, "How would you feel if some maniac on a motorcycle cut you off in traffic?" actually ended up winning the Starboyz' affections, as the piece ended up prompting more and more high-profile media coverage, including a spot on the UPN network's *Real TV*—a segment that is included in *FTP 2 1/2*.

Of course, as the news cameras continued to roll, so did the sales figures for *FTP 1*. "If I could find that reporter, I'd give her a big hug and kiss because that news report was how we finally got known all across the country," Marino said.

However, it wasn't long after the Fox News story ran that the Starboyz experienced a fierce crackdown from police who threatened to permanently end their fun. For certain, there are better ways to get to know the local police than having your mug splashed on the nightly news for riding three-mile stand-up wheelies in traffic.

The Big Time and Beyond

If you ask the Starboyz just when they hit the big time, most will tell you it happened about two weeks after the news profile. That's when Kevin and Lisa Marino woke up to find an Akron City Police cruiser parked just outside their door. "I woke up and saw this guy just sitting there, like, for hours, and then I called Scott and Joe and they each had one too," Marino said. Suddenly, it became harder and harder to ride anywhere, be it to the corner store for a 40-ounce bottle of Bull or to the shop for new tires. "They were all over us. Every time we hit the roads we were getting pulled over and hassled," Marino said.

The roads were still where it was happening, but offers for shows were staring to become harder and harder for the Starboyz to pass up after the 1999 release of *FTP 2*. At first, the team had no idea of the level of their

Once thrown out of the AMA's Pickerington, Ohio, headquarters, in 2001 the Starboyz were invited to perform at the AMA Superbike races at the Mid-Ohio Sportscar Course. The passenger almost meets the asphalt with this stunt, created by England's Gary Rothwell.

Stunts and other things that hundreds of times had nearly gotten the Starboyz arrested suddenly had the whole world beating a path to their door.

International influence? A British Starboyz' fan, replete with customized Mylar leathers, at an Akron, Ohio, sportbike hangout. *Performance Bike Magazine/Emap Publishing*

popularity or how to assess a value to something they'd been doing for years just for fun. Early shows found them running full, 30-minute performances for new tires and a hot meal; other shows were done just for the trophies—and girls.

Early shows found them running full, 30-minute performances for new tires and a hot meal; other shows were done just for the trophies—and girls.

By 1999, the Starboyz had headlined the Night Under Fire at Ohio's Norwalk Dragway, where they performed for a crowd of some 30,000 and met the heavyweight boxing champion of the time, Michael Moorer, who, as it turned out, was a sportbike enthusiast and serious Starboyz fan.

The footage from Norwalk ended up in *FTP 2*, a rollicking, action-intense 50 minutes of street extreme video. While a legion of imitators have fallen into the habit of simply recording a few stunts on a favorite practice road, *FTP 2* is a wild travelogue of the Starboyz' season. There's a three-up stoppie achieved—with a young lady, naturally, sandwiched in between Marino and Frazier—at Myrtle Beach and several smoky burnouts that end with the ear-popping burst of a rear tire.

This is a favorite trick of part-time Starboy, "Big Dave" Sonsky. Recently, he's begun experimenting with adding everything from shredded Starboyz posters to tiny glitter stars inside his rear tire's rim. After a long, nasty burnout, Sonsky presents the fans with a star-studded explosion.

The *FTP 2* video ended up winning one of Impact Video's "Extremy Awards" at the 2000 Indianapolis Motorsports Dealer Exposition in recognition of its constantly changing locales and scary incidents that can only happen on the streets.

At one point, a camera car rides alongside Marino as he maintains a steady wheelie that manages to pull away from the chase car even as the Camaro's speedometer shows 125. While the lens focuses on Marino's motorcycle, a yellow blur appears briefly, obscuring the view of his bike, then disappears.

"That was a car," Marino explained. He'd been concentrating so intently on keeping the wheelie lofted while the cameraman struggled to stay with the bike, Marino never noticed that his bike had drifted across the double-yellow line and into oncoming traffic. "The car brushed my foot off the peg and just kept going. I was too hyped about the wheelie to really care," he said.

What do the Starboyz and other street extreme teams want more than fame and excitement? Perhaps a tire sponsor. This is the result of one day's rehearsal session. Starboy Joe Frazier makes weekly trips to bike repair shops where he pleads for discarded street tires that have "a little life left in 'em."

Longtime cameraman and editor Jon Hayes shot most of *FTP 2,* and even captured a police cruiser as it lazily followed the Starboyz' bikes down a country highway—even though the bikes were secured to a trailer. Leftover footage from these shoots and some new taping ended up in *FTP 2 ¹/2,* a shorter collection of roadside chaos that's nearly as much fun as its predecessor.

Better All the Time

In time, the Starboyz' level of skill improved alongside the performance fees. Because the long, stand-up wheelies that thrilled 'em on the expressways proved impossible in a controlled environment, Caraboolad started working on slower, more precise wheelstands, while Marino perfected two-up stoppies with willing (and brave) passenger Tave Stanley clinging to the pillion seat. Burnout and standing-start wheelie king Frazier, who had been injured in one of the team's occasional accidents, drifted away for a while, replaced by Sonsky, who is clearly one of the sport's rising stars.

Last year, England's *Super Bike* magazine caught up with the Starboyz at Daytona Beach Bike Week, and Sonsky stole the show by planting his 6-foot, 4-inch, 240-pound frame atop the handlebars of his tiger-striped CBR 900 and popping a wheelie that was almost completely vertical. That he did so in front of a charging semi-trailer on a bike with burping oil lines and two flat spots on the front wheel has only added to his reputation as one bad mutha.

> He'd been concentrating so intently that Marino **never noticed that his bike had drifted across the double-yellow line** and into oncoming traffic.

Sonsky stole the show by planting his 6-foot, 4-inch, 240-pound frame atop the handlebars and popping a wheelie that was almost completely vertical.

SHOWTIME

After so many years together, there's cohesiveness to the Starboyz' performances that can only come with countless rehearsals. When they launch into a set of rolling, sideways burnouts, the bikes nearly veer into each other again and again, but each rider seems to know precisely how to spin around the other. A big part of the Starboyz' show involves a series of increasingly steep-angled stoppies and switchbacks, with riders contorting themselves from forward to backward and back again, all the while keeping the throttle pinned. Sometimes working in small confines barely big enough to build up speed, they've somehow managed to avoid collisions while intentionally coming within inches of the next bike. It could easily turn disastrous, but doesn't, Frazier said, only because of how long and frequently the boyz have rehearsed.

OUTLAWS OR PROS?

By 2000, the Starboyz were finding it harder to maintain the dual role of outlaws and professional stunt riders. Sure, their real fans still wanted to see them escape a good police chase or drift past cars on one wheel, but the consequences of street riding were less and less attractive all the time.

This became particularly clear after a Friday-night show at the National Trails Raceway outside of Columbus. The crew headed for a nearby motel, riding stand-up wheelies at around 90 miles per hour for miles on the Columbus thoroughfare. Now, after holding a long-distance wheelie for about four miles, the sump on a sportbike motor begins to spew a fine mist of oil as low-end pressure builds when oil drains backward from the oil-starved engine head. The spray was slowly coating Sonsky's rear tire, and as Caraboolad noticed, Sonsky set the CBR's front Dunlop down with a loud chirp and blast of blue smoke. The guys all had a decent laugh about that one later, and decided to try it again the following morning.

On that day, both Marino and Caraboolad doused their wheelies and gunned their engines as the too-familiar sound of a police siren wailed from about 100 yards back. As Marino made a run for it, Caraboolad pulled over for the state trooper, who was joined by a woman in a late-model Ford Escort. The female motorist had called the state police on her cellular phone, and she stood by the roadside demanding that Caraboolad be arrested for pulling a wheelie. The cop let Caraboolad go with a warning, and Marino, who perpetually has more points on his license than a Laker's scoreboard, spent the next two hours riding dirt back roads and even pulling into a barn to escape another ticket. "After that, we pretty much started trucking our bikes to shows," Caraboolad said.

Sonsky set the CBR's front Dunlop down with a loud chirp and blast of blue smoke.

Problem solved, right? Even when stunt riders transport their motorcycles to shows on the backs of flatbed trucks and trailers, their very presence can attract police cars. In Brooklyn Heights, a suburb of Akron, several stunt riders who had gathered for the Starboyz' Summer 2001 Stunt Festival were trading ideas and practicing a few moves when a police cruiser rolled in just seconds after Team X-Treem stunt rider Derrick "D-Mann" Daigle set down his front end. The officer pulled into the Holiday Inn parking lot where the stunt riders had parked their trailers and support vehicles and instantly started barking about "impounding motorcycles and confiscating cameras."

Cy J. Cyr

Daigle, who works as a firefighter when he's not performing at stunt shows, soon convinced the officer that the situation was under control. The officer explained that he'd been briefed by his superiors about the Starboyz and other motorcycle stunt riders, and had come expecting the worst. Before he left, the officer shook hands with a few riders, grabbed a few souvenir videotapes, and even convinced rider Ronnie Giovelli, of Deer Park Long Island's Reality Racing, to pull a few seat-stand wheelies—with police permission, of course. Giovelli, whose arms and back are covered in thick scabs and scars from four years of shirtless stunt riding, was more than happy to oblige.

Even when stunt riders transport their motorcycles to shows on the backs of flatbed trucks and trailers, their very presence can attract police cars.

"I don't have anything against you guys doing your thing, but the problems we see are kids who aren't that talented, trying to get out on the public roads and imitate the Starboyz. I've seen kids hurt out here on motorcycles that were just way too fast for kids with this little experience," the officer explained.

The decision to trade street riding for solely performing at paid shows was not entirely made because of the cops, the Starboyz will tell you. When talking about the perceived and real dangers of street extreme, Frazier said the most dangerous part of riding street is other bikers. "When we go somewhere like Daytona Beach (where the Starboyz have performed at several Bike Week celebrations) there are always riders who want to ride with us or tape us to see up close how we ride. That's when it gets scary: Somebody always gets in the way or runs into somebody."

Marino, who was clipped from behind by a biker while pulling a legs-spread, sitting-on-the-gas-tank wheelie through a busy Daytona intersection, and later, T-boned by an awestruck teenager in Miami, more than agrees. "We've been doing this for so long, and practiced it so many hundreds of times, it's safe. It's people who don't know what they're doing that scare me." Marino contends that street extreme riding is "not that dangerous, compared to other types of things you can do on a sportbike." He's famous for a story he tells when asked why the Starboyz don't include a cornering display in their shows. "A bunch of us had been reading *Performance Bike* and all these English magazines where everybody has their knees down in the turns, so we decided to try it for ourselves. Man, after about four turns, we ended up with people laying all over the road, bones broken, bikes busted apart, on fire, and people laying all over the road like a scene in a war movie. It was gnarly," he laughed.

For a group of guys who've been tanked and ridden on top of vans with very little clothing on, wheelied across the Florida Keys on a low-level bridge *(FTP 2),* and reached 154 miles per hour on one wheel, the Starboyz refuse to acknowledge any danger in street extreme. When given new $700 Arai helmets by a sponsor, Caraboolad and Sonsky ended up rolling theirs down the Thompson Raceway in a game of high-speed helmet bowling. Vanson leathers chimed in during the 2001 season with offers of free, customized gear, but all four Starboyz declined to don the padded leather pants favored by Europe's professional stunt riders. "I ain't goin' out looking like some geek in AMA Superbike. I'm not crashin' anyway," joked Marino, who's most comfortable in a T-shirt, baggy jeans, and Vans sneakers. "If I'm not laying on the street, bleeding out of my butt, or puking up solid objects, I'm not suiting up or going to the hospital," Frazier said.

When given new $700 Arai helmets by a sponsor, Caraboolad and Sonsky ended up **rolling theirs down the Thompson Raceway in a game of high-speed helmet bowling.**

Chapter 3

A Movement
Is Born

Just as the Starboyz spent the better part of 1997 staring a hole into their television sets as they studied the moves and technique of Gary Rothwell in *Showtime,* dozens of others sportbike riders were busy studying that tape as well. Two years later, after the Starboyz shocked the motorcycling community with the release of *FTP 1,* more and more local wheelie kings and would-be stunt heroes began emulating that tape with similar intensity.

Talk with street extreme riders today and you'll quickly realize that those early videocassettes are considered the all-inspiring Old Testament of street extreme—hallowed texts to be studied, emulated, and virtually worshipped by a legion of would-be Rothwells.

"I'd been riding wheelies for a couple of years—maybe holding one for a block or two. Then I saw Rothwell's tape and thought, 'Damn, this stuff goes farther than I ever imagined.' The more guys I showed that tape to, the more people you started seeing out on the streets trying to do wheelies and stuff," said Dan Urban, of Wisconsin's D-Aces.

Todd Colbert

Tampa's Todd Colbert was among those who happened upon Rothwell's *Showtime* by chance and couldn't believe someone was being paid to do what he'd been doing in traffic for years. Colbert is a tall and lanky veteran street rider who, in his early 30s, is one of the senior statesmen of the street extreme movement. He's the sport's Tony Hawk, having elevated the profile of streetbike stunt riding through dozens of professional shows, major industry sponsorships, and Hollywood stunt work.

The man behind an entire movement: England's Gary Rothwell. Though Rothwell is one of the best-known names in international stunt riding, he too got his start performing illegally on the streets.

G-Nice, of New Jersey's Ruthless Tactics, goes nose down at a local drag strip.

Rothwell's smooth, professional approach to stunt riding so inspired Colbert that his main stuntbike is a full-on replica of the British streetfighter-style machine that Rothwell has ridden for the past 10 years. It's a juiced-up mid-1990s Suzuki GSX-R1100, outfitted with motocross handlebars and upgraded suspension to defer those hard landings. "I've always liked the British guys and the Europeans, like A. C. Farias, because they seem to have a real fine level of control to their

Already well-known throughout the Tampa area for his particularly inspired street riding, Colbert was first asked to perform stunts at an Indy Car race in 1995.

Gary Rothwell went after the American stunt market and several Guinness World Records, including longest stoppie and most persons on a wheelie (13 and counting!). *Brian J. Nelson*

stunts. They run a clean show and really know how to give the crowd what they want," Colbert said.

Already well-known throughout the Tampa area for his particularly in-spired street riding, Colbert was first asked to perform stunts at an Indy car race in 1995. The crowd reaction that day told Colbert that he'd happened upon a skill that most motorsports enthusiasts had never seen but were ready to support. That spring came the first of many Daytona 200 appear-

Big T" Todd Colbert twists up a sidewinder stoppie on his tricked-out Suzuki GSX-R750. Colbert can actually run this move into a wheelie without chopping the throttle.

ances. By summer, offers to perform at drag strips throughout the South were streaming in and Colbert soon found his time split between practicing his stunts and gearing up for busy weekends.

Although he can be seen in his videos, *Urban Assault* and *Moving Violations,* trippin' out rush-hour commuters with long, rolling burnouts on the steamy streets of Florida, Colbert always rehearses off-road. He's been fortunate to have had access to a local airstrip for practicing his craft; without the hassles and potential pitfalls of traffic to deal with, he's managed to perfect some fairly incredible stunts. Rolling stoppies that end in twisting, 180-degree turns, and the fabled "Ghost Ride," where Colbert helps Daigle actually surf in front of a rolling motorcycle in order to remount a riderless bike are but two of the moves that have left Colbert's name all over the industry's lips.

Colbert, who has appeared alone and with his former wife, Lori, in a half-dozen street extreme videotapes, is organizing an annual amateur stunt rider's competition to be held at Daytona International Speedway during the spring Bike Week rally. His Team X-Treem has helped launch the careers of some of the sport's hot young stars including J. T. Holt, who has also worked as a professional stuntman for Universal Orlando. Always the consummate professional who never performs without a helmet or leathers, Colbert's training regimen includes studying martial arts, which explains his signature move—seat-stands while twirling nunchakus.

Colbert believes controlled stunt shows in closed environments are the best thing to happen to street extreme in recent years.

Though he can recall a time not too long ago when he and the Tampa Police Department were better acquainted than he would ever wish, Colbert believes controlled stunt shows in closed environments are the best thing to happen to street extreme in recent years. "I think moving off the streets is smart because it frees us up to concentrate on riding instead of getting hurt or getting busted. I mean, everybody who's doing this has had their problems riding on the street. I know that people like seeing me do the street stuff, especially in the videos, but I honestly feel like this sport is going forward, and getting it recognized as a legitimate sport, like freestyle motocross, BMX, or any of those is going to take organization and events," he said.

Performing on the streets also brings into play the unavoidable imitations from less skilled riders.

Other well-known street extreme riders couldn't agree more. Pauly Sherer, a founding member of Las Vegas Extremes (LVX), has, in his words, "been trying to move the sport in a safer, more respectable direction," for years. He wholeheartedly supports the formation of Colbert's U.S. Stunt Riding Championships and SFX Entertainment's XSBA.

"If Las Vegas Extremes goes out for a ride and we film some onboard footage, we pick one of the safest back roads with a good, clear approach and exit, and even that's sometimes not safe enough. The thing I've seen a thousand times on stunt videos is riders going out and just blazing away regardless of traffic, and that's a major problem. If they just allow traffic to pass, they can probably get away with it for a lot longer because those same drivers you like to pass doing a stand-up wheelie are the same drivers who'll call the cops. Sure, we basically started out on the streets, too, but if SFX is going to support what we do and authenticate us and show us to new audiences then, as riders, we're going to support what they're doing," Sherer said.

Performing on the streets also brings into play the unavoidable imitations from less-skilled riders. Sure, if it weren't for imitation, Colbert wouldn't have been inspired by Rothwell, and Rothwell wouldn't have been prompted to leave Wales to pursue a stunt career after watching winning Grand Prix racers fool around on one wheel following races. But after a March 2000 performance at Daytona Fun Machines (which was captured in the excellent compilation video *Road Rage*), one rider who tried to outdo Colbert ended up looping his Suzuki TL1000S sport twin during an overzealous wheelie and was seriously injured in the process.

Such incidents aren't uncommon. Scott Caraboolad, of Akron's Starboyz, recalled a disastrous weekend invitation to ride with a fledgling stunt crew in Long Island, New York. Little did the Starboyz know, the road where this crew practiced had been the site of a deadly chase in which a Long Island patrolman was killed pursuing one of the stunt riders just months before.

"I pull one wheelie and five seconds later, there's flashing lights everywhere and cops threatening to shoot us. I mean, these guys needed to show the cops some respect and use their heads. The only thing worse we

Cy J. Cyr

could have done was go to the cemetery where this cop was buried and do burnouts on his grave, for Christ's sake," Caraboolad said.

Still, Colbert is fully encouraging of younger riders entering the sport. His annual U.S. Stunt Rider's Association competition is intended as a means for "guys who don't have the money or the contacts to put an internationally distributed tape out to get themselves some exposure." Best of all, the Daytona show will not be staged as a brief halftime show between road races, Colbert is quick to point out, but will headline as its own freestanding event. "What I'm basically trying to do is raise the profile of street extreme to a point where the U.S. magazines can't ignore it any longer. If I can pull together all of these riders and groups that don't have representation and get them noticed, it's good for everybody," he said.

Las Vegas Extremes

Like Colbert, Derrick "D-Mann" Daigle's background in stunt work and more than 20 years spent studying martial arts helped this Las Vegas resident and fire truck driver immeasurably when it came to busting street moves. But where years of Ninjutsu training helped with balance and muscle control, Daigle's work as a professional Jet Ski racer and stunt performer was the best thing to happen to wheelies since the invention of the Kevlar clutch. "I started off riding a Honda 50 when I was just five years old, and I was on the circuit racing Jet Skis for five years off and on when I started street riding and doing stunts. I realized right away when I got on my first streetbike that I had an advantage as far as balance was concerned," Daigle said.

> Daigle's work as a professional Jet Ski racer and stunt performer was **the best thing to happen to wheelies** since the invention of the Kevlar clutch.

The affable, well-read 29-year-old said that he ingested the same early street extreme influences as the Starboyz and Colbert: Rothwell's *Showtime* video, *Performance Bikes, SuperBike, Streetfighters*, and other cutting-edge British sportbike magazines. In 1996, Daigle met up with Ofer Nurkin and Pauly Sherer, two like-minded Las Vegas street riders who were themselves exploring the limits of physics and gravity. The trio bought a small, helmet-mounted camera and

Las Vegas Extremes front man Pauly Sherer: businessman, filmmaker, and one of the world's best stunt riders. *LVX Photography*

Fast fashions from Riders 4 Life. In a 2001 newspaper article in the *Cleveland Scene*, members confessed to being "like Evel Knievel, but the shit we do is illegal."

spent the next 18 months perfecting and recording a very polished, highly spectacular series of stunts.

The team, which became known as Las Vegas Extremes (LVX), found a unique niche in the then-fledgling street extreme movement. It didn't hurt that the eye-popping urban scenery of the Las Vegas Strip and bizarre visual contrasts of the Southern Nevada desert lent LVX's premiere tape a dramatic quality that's seldom been matched. Riding nac-nac wheelies past startled tourists along the Strip and taking full advantage of Nevada's wide-open boulevards also assisted in the creation of some of LVX's signature stunts, including Sketching, or the art of skiing behind and beside a bike for miles on end.

The eye-popping urban scenery of the Las Vegas Strip and bizarre visual contrasts of the Southern Nevada desert lent LVX's premiere tape a dramatic quality.

Derrick "D-Mann" Daigle, dressed for success and the possibility of a high-speed dismount. Daigle is one of street extreme's leading ambassadors, linking the world of outlaws with the world of show business.

Sherer, who is blessed with the twin gifts of gab and steady nerves, perfected the Standing Christ, a move that involves a full stand from the saddle, with arms extended. The team is also known for achieving tank-mounted head- and hand-stands, and Daigle performs an unbelievable move he calls the Leap of Faith, where he jumps from the seat of his pristine Suzuki GSX-R750 to the gas tank and back again.

Chaindrive's J. T. Holt sharpens his one-handed wheelie skills with Starboy Scott Caraboolad in hot pursuit.

"I'll admit that where we live really had a lot to do with how our program developed. The city of Las Vegas is laid out on a grid, and there are hardly any corners, so if you want to learn roadracing moves or drag your knee in corners, there's nowhere to do that. We got bored easily and realized that we could either develop a riding style for those kinds of roads or give up riding. It was that simple," Sherer said. The roads were so long, straight, and uninterrupted by cross-traffic, Sherer said, that LVX riders could practice rolling endoes (or stoppies) and blend that move into a roaring wheelie without ever having to be concerned with intersections or traffic.

As with other street extreme riders, Daigle reveals no deep psychological underpinnings for choosing motorcycle stunt riding as a vocation. He attributes his choice of careers to the all-consuming demon of boredom. "Coming from the background of having done Jet Ski stunts, I get bored really easily. I was riding my bike one day and just thought to myself, 'How long can I pull a wheelie?' I ended up doing like a 20-minute wheelie between Las Vegas and Laughlin (Nevada) at 140 miles per hour, and I decided right then that I was either going to start riding stunts professionally or quit riding, because stunts were clearly the most fun," he said.

LVX certainly helped the movement along by simply displaying photos of their stunts on their Web site. Later, as they advertised their weekend shows in the parking lots of restaurants and gas stations around Las Vegas, the Web site eventually became one of the team's greatest assets. "We just had a site that said 'Come see our extreme riding in Las Vegas' (hence the name) and these lame pictures of us learning stunts. But people were showing up from all across the country, e-mailing us to say they were coming in to Vegas to see us. We didn't know what to think," Sherer said.

LVX's first video, *Las Vegas Extremes*, even contains a couple of spectacular crashes, including a hard-to-watch flip-over wheelie where Sherer ends up with a major scalping.

It was all pretty heady stuff and LVX's first video, *Las Vegas Extremes,* even contains a couple of spectacular crashes, including a hard-to-watch flipover wheelie where Sherer ends up with a major scalping. In between the stunts, LVX sandwiched a few dirty jokes and some good-humored fun with midget bikes and unsuspecting waitresses. Few teams have been as innovative and have yet to energize the sport as thoughtfully and radically as LVX. Current LVX team leader Sherer (Daigle now performs alone or with Team X-Treem) said the trio is aware that their program is different from the stunts they'd seen performed by others and they expect a healthy response to their tape.

The competition heats up for real as Tave Stanley—sometime-Starboy and freelance stunt rider—shows class with the gas-charged flamethrower on his Honda CBR.

Sherer, who speaks with the unabashed cockiness of a youthful Muhammad Ali, was shocked to see 10,000 copies of *Las Vegas Extremes* sell in its first two months following release in October 1998.

Sherer, who speaks with the unabashed cockiness of a youthful Muhammad Ali, was shocked to see 10,000 copies of *Las Vegas Extremes* sell in its first two months following release in October 1998. The video grossed some $250,000 in sales, mostly achieved via word of mouth. "We were about the first team to really break big in this country. Everybody who came after us has pretty much imitated us," Sherer said.

Today, Sherer runs LVX like a small, tightly wound corporation. Shows at AMA Superbike races have replaced the nightly forays down the Las Vegas Strip, and the team spends most of each year on the road. Instead of relying on a familiar lineup of riders, Sherer said seeking out and showcasing new talents is what LVX is all about. "I get the impression people assumed that the first LVX lineup was the permanent team, but LVX was just the title and, just like Team Yoshimura Suzuki, the members are constantly changing. It's an entirely different approach from, say, what the Starboyz are doing, but it's our belief that people want to see new guys bringing in new stunts," he said.

His aluminum foil–covered Suzuki GSX-R1000 revving toward the redline, Paul Marmorato of New York's Finest executes a feet-up donut. Later, he raises one hand, rodeo style.

With so many young punters trying their hand at the street extreme game, Sherer said LVX picks up new riders through videotaped submissions, inside references, or just by running into riders displaying raw, fearless talent out on the streets. "I've gotta say I like the guys who are willing to really stick their necks out and take chances. The guy other people may not want to ride with because he may be considered dangerous, that's our man. I always say, if a guy's not crashing, he's not learning," he said.

Daigle, who helped revolutionize and broaden the repertoire of street extreme stunts, advised new riders to diversify and try all sorts of sports before hitting the streets. "If you've ever seen Jet Skis racing, or Jet Skiers playing around doing freestyle, you'd know that just about everything I invented in *Las Vegas Extremes* was from Jet Skis. There's all sorts of stuff you learn to do on the water in a freestyle Jet Ski competition, like skiing backwards on the water and bulldogging, which is when you fly off to the side of the ski. Well, when I got interested in riding streetbikes a couple of years later, the moves like what Jet Skiers call the Porpoise, where you blast up through the water and stand the ski on its rear, they turned out to be way easier on a bike," he said.

Two-up riding from Florida's Broward Boyz. This furred-out Suzuki TL1000S Twin is a mainstay of stunt riding for its easily accessible torque.

Daigle advised new riders to diversify and try all sorts of sports before hitting the streets.

Oddly, while it would seem the unforgiving texture of asphalt would make for a tougher playing field than water, Daigle said his stunts appear so smooth because paved roadways don't undulate the way lakes and rivers do. Similarly, he'd already learned how to whip his legs around and over the handlebars of a Jet Ski well enough that motorcycle handlebar-stands were second nature by the time Daigle made the transition to street riding. "That's the biggest danger in any handlebar-seated stuff like rolling stoppies from the bars—being able to get up there and not upset the controls by accidentally whacking your knees against the bars," he said.

Sherer, for his part, is one of the few stunt experts who attributes his success to "falling down too much and practicing as much as I can, but still not enough." It helps that Sherer, stocky and muscular, has an undeniable level of natural athletic ability and a lengthy background in amateur roadracing. Working with Mike Cicotto's Hooters Team Suzuki, he claimed a third- and fourth-place finish at Loudon in CCS Superbike racing in 2000.

After completing their tape and making it available in bike shops throughout the Southwest, LVX received a call from independent producer Steve Abbot from the renowned *Crusty Demons of Dirt* video series. Abbott turned X-Factor video producer Eric Lee on to LVX and, in months, the trio was fielding offers to perform throughout the region, Daigle said. The group's first show, at a Las Vegas Hooters Restaurant, cemented in his mind the idea of stunt riding professionally.

"They had something called the Badass Bike Shoot-Out of 1999 and we showed up to do our thing and there were all these Harley people and serious outlaw bikers lined up," Daigle said. Despite the very non-performance-oriented crowd, he said the overwhelmingly positive audience response showed LVX that a market for stunt shows definitely exists. "One of these guys from the Vagos, this outlaw biker club, walked up and smiled and said, 'Man that was sick.' That proved to me that people—all kinds of riders—can appreciate stunt riding."

Feet up and spinning, the circle burnout is fun, but it often alerts law enforcement to the so-called "hot roads" where stunt teams practice. Within a matter of weeks, or sometimes days, these roads can be shut down without warning.

All Yamaha YZFR1 all the time: The Miami Warriors, a Jamaican street extreme group that's making headway in the South.

What's in a name? Rob Marley, son of late reggae giant Bob Marley, balances his stunt craft with his singing career. Once in place, Marley can ride in this position for miles. "The only thing that gets tired is your wrists. You have to be ready for that."

THE LAS VEGAS EXTREMES AND FTP 1 LEGACY

In the fiercely competitive world of street extreme, there's no shortage of people who claim to have single-handedly launched the sport, with LVX's Sherer being among the most vocal.

Closer to the truth, like many pop culture movements before it, is that street extreme grew simultaneously from several wellsprings. Kids in Topeka, Kansas, might have met stunt riders from Toronto who just happened to have seen the same videos and attempted the same stunts. In a matter of months, a movement was taking shape that exhibited a shared riding style, dress code, and streetwise sensibility where every rider was determined to one-up the last guy.

Reaching the market only a few months apart, *Las Vegas Extremes* and *FTP 1* paved the way for the deluge of self-produced street extreme videos now available.

As with Rothwell and the Starboyz, the power of a homemade videotape to pass the word along to newcomers and continually reinvigorate street extreme with new, innovative stunts proved to be the stepping-stone LVX needed. Checks were pouring in as the tape continued to sell

Even the best-laid plans sometimes get out of hand. This rider managed to save his 180-degree stoppie, but just barely. The crash-damaged frame protector says this is not the first mishap this rider has encountered.

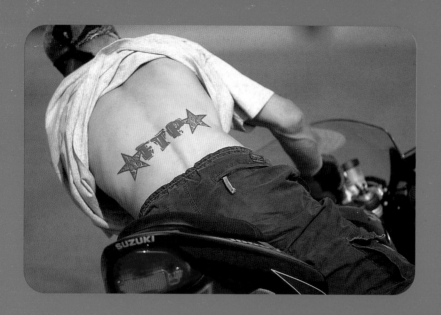

briskly throughout the late 1990s. Sponsors lined up, offering everything from Hindle exhaust systems and Motul oils to free repair work and much-needed replacement plastic body parts from Airtech.

Reaching the market only a few months apart, *Las Vegas Extremes* and *FTP 1* paved the way for the deluge of self-produced street extreme videos now available. Now that the members of LVX have ridden off in separate directions, Daigle performs alone or with Colbert's Team X-Treem. He's been busy performing his stunts across the United States and England and was recently drafted to boost stoppies in a 2002 Nissan commercial. Today Daigle is among those who are glad to see major video distributors, such as California's X-Factor and Impact Video, promoting street extreme.

Daigle is among those who are glad to see major video distributors, such as California's X-Factor and Impact Video, promoting street extreme.

"When *Las Vegas Extremes* came out it was a phenomenon. I mean, we were coming up with things nobody had ever seen before. I can't say I was the first person to do this stuff because if you really research street extreme, you'll find out that way back in the day there were old, old-school Harley guys who had done some really insane shit like The Elevator, where they would jump from the foot pegs all the way to the gas tank, and this was on bikes with no suspension. But they didn't have video distributors making their stuff known and getting it seen all over the world, like we do," he said.

Looking back, Daigle said experience as a video producer has taught him that *Las Vegas Extremes* could have been completed in four

"The main problem with staging amateur stunt shows is the amateurs," joked Derrick "D-Mann" Daigle. Case in point: a rider clearly more familiar with stoppies on video than in action rolls into the crowded staging area at Thompson Dragway. His stoppie starts a high-speed wobble and, Wham! Into the crowd. In the foreground, recovering from a collision with the rolling Kawasaki, is Starboy Joe Frazier, who had already been out injured for several months.

weeks rather than two years. Yet his advice to amateurs is to, "Take your time and get it right. We would get excited that we'd gotten a stunt right, and we'd spend all day doing it for the cameras, only when we got back home to watch the footage, we'd end up with four hours of clouds or roadway close-ups because we were so stupid. We'd set the camera up wrong or we'd end up forgetting how it would shift. Now, I check the camera every few minutes," he laughed.

After checking his camera, Daigle is a stickler for checking out any damage sustained to his always-pristine Suzuki GSX-R1000. He said that a clean, polished-out motorcycle demands more awe from an audience, and admits that having sponsors and a few years under his belt helps keep a stuntbike looking like something that's just been rolled into a show room. "If I crash my bike, which has happened, I just won't ride it until it's been fixed," Daigle said. Suzuki's GSX-Rs, whether in 600-, 750-, or the new 1000-cc format, seem to be the most prevalent bikes in street extreme, something Daigle attributes to the bulletproof reliability and wickedly broad powerbands. "It's all right there—top end for the skis and high-speed roadwork and enough torque to really whack it for a wheelie. Even the front ends don't complain a lot after you wheelie, and the brakes are about as good as stock brakes get," he said.

Sherer, with his keen eye for business opportunity, has taken the street extreme movement's love affair with Suzuki's fours to the source.

> Suzuki's GSX-Rs, whether in 600-, 750-, or the new 1000-cc format, seem to be **the most prevalent bikes in street extreme.**

Quads may be the lazy man's stuntbike, but fully chromed and customized four-wheelers have become a staple of the street stunt scene.

He developed a close enough relationship with Suzuki Motor Corporation that he was granted permission to film his crew doing burnouts and stoppies inside a Team Suzuki tent at the Laguna Seca World Superbike races in 2000. In addition, GP roadracing legend and Suzuki Team Yoshimura Coach Kevin Schwantz is expected to make an appearance in an upcoming LVX video.

After watching the street extreme movement grow from a smattering of self-produced tapes of kids running from the cops and breaking their butts, Daigle is optimistic that today's riders are on the cusp of something bigger than most of them can imagine. "I honestly believe we are right where dirt bikes were five years ago. I mean, yeah, there's still resistance and people who think we're all outlaws or we're all crazy, but every new sport meets a level of resistance until the mainstream accepts it and realizes how much money they could potentially make from it. We might even be maybe a few miles ahead of them because they just popped up recently, but stunt riding motorcycles is really already in the mainstream when you look at major movies like *Mission Impossible II.* "Once people see what's possible from a talented rider on a crotch rocket, it's endless what can be done. There are kids right now, all over the country, learning different ways to do stunts and I think eventually, if they get enough exposure, it will boggle the public's mind. In the next three years, street extreme will explode," he said.

"This will be bigger than the Gravity Games someday, I can guarantee it, Sherer said. "We're helping the motorsports industry along and they know it."

Pop in the Tape

One symbiotic relationship that cannot be denied is the link between video distribution houses and the exponential growth of street stunt riding. Among the most notable have been X-Factor Video and Impact Video, both located in California. Impact owner and producer Docy Andrews brings a background in public relations, theater management, and acting to the table, and today, Impact offers hundreds of videos covering everything from BMX, dirt bikes, watercraft, and snowboarding.

Though freestyle motocross tapes and videos that capture the wackier side of dirt riding remain the industry leaders, street extreme is now the fastest-growing segment of the business, Andrews said. The release

> Though freestyle motocross tapes and videos that capture the wackier side of dirt riding remain the industry leaders, street extreme is now the fastest-growing segment of the business.

of over 30 tapes in just two years has helped Impact grow from a small, one-woman show based in Andrews' home to a 13-person business in a 3,500-square-foot Laguna Hills facility.

Many of the early street extreme tapes that enthusiasts have come to respect and imitate are in fairly rough form and are a few hours of home-video footage and musical soundtrack desperately in need of editorial direction. Impact sets riders up with producers and editors who turn that raw, "look out for the squad car," footage into pure entertainment. Andrews said that lately the genre seems to be growing up, with teams submitting more professionally shot footage. The grainy, unsteady handy-cam shots that characterized the Starboyz' *FTP 1,* for example, are rare these days and even the youngest riders are concentrating on digital cameras, multiple-angle shots, and slick, clean editing. Andrews also expects the recent staging of sanctioned stunt shows to eventually

"Yeah, I sort of do feel like somebody's been watching me," thought Reality Racing's Ronnie Giovelli.

Cy J. Cyr

result in street extreme tapes that resemble freestyle motocross videos in quality of content.

"When the genre first got started, it was just street riders basically shooting their own stuff and putting it on tape. In most of the other extreme sports, you have enthusiasts who are not a featured element of their own videos. Whether you're looking at a skateboard, dirt bike, or snowboarding video, the guys who are really enthusiasts and producers, they don't really get involved in competition so much anymore as they direct their energies shooting everyone else. What's happening now with street extreme is this genre is growing up a bit, and you'll see more producers shooting other riders for compilation tapes, like Todd Colbert seems to be doing already," she said.

Andrews decided last year to reward and recognize the hard work involved in producing a street extreme video by launching the Impact Video Extremy Awards at the Indianapolis Motorsports Dealer Expo. Hoping to credit a segment of the motorsports community that is too often ignored or outright dissed by the often middle-aged magazine editors and media officials, the Extremys, Andrews said, brings disparate elements of the motorsports family together for some synergy and much-needed networking. "I started out my career as a producer and I know all about the sacrifice, money, heart, and hours you put into something like this for, what is a lot of times, very little in return," she said.

The Impact Video Extremy Awards **brings disparate elements of the motorsports family together for some synergy** and much-needed networking.

X-Factor's Chris Lee actually operates something of an in-house video-tape production facility in his Orange County, California, headquarters. Instead of linking would-be stunt legends up with producers or editors, X-Factor develops raw footage on the premises, adds music, and packages tapes before they make their way into the marketplace. X-Factor's 2000 release, *Full Leather Jacket,* starring Chaindrive, of Orlando, Florida, has proven to be one of the most popular street extreme releases in recent years. Lee credits "his" talented stable of riders with making X-Factor a huge international presence in the sport.

> "When we were filming for our video, and **things got dull, I'd just dream up some sick shit and do it.**" —*Ryan Bonneau, Chaindrive*

"There are lots of guys out there who are good riders and may know how to push the record button on a Palmcorder and pull impressive wheelies, but when it comes to marketing themselves, sometimes it just doesn't work. That's what we do," said Lee, who also had a hand in bringing the stunt team New York's Finest and *All Twisted and Pucked Up,* which features an all-star cast of riders and is the first corner-carving video, to the screen.

Even as the marketing arm and acceptance of street extreme continues to grow, new talents continue to be created on the streets. This fact is not lost on Impact's Andrews, who remains open to seeing works from new riders. She warns, however, that tapes containing little more than endless repetitive shots of riders pulling wheelies along a deserted industrial access road won't cut it anymore. "I'd say the most important value (in a street extreme video) is in what's being shown. Is it interesting and innovative? Is it funny and does it show things in a different slant or does it show you something you don't see every day? That's what people are looking for," she said.

Show 'Em Something New: Chaindrive

In late 1997, MTV aired a new type of program. It starred a gangly, sometimes incoherent former public access cable TV host from Canada named Tom Green. Green was the hapless everyman taken to extremes: Not only did things on his program never quite go as planned, he was often a willing participant in a series of increasingly horrendous stunts and awful pranks that inevitably went wrong. Two years later, Green's show was a hit, and MTV rushed other similar, reality-based programming into production.

One of the wildest was *Jackass,* a no-limits half-hour program where the guileless host was paid to subject himself to the types of stomach-turning dares and pranks usually concocted after a long night around a keg. J. T. Holt, Ryan Bonneau, and Adam Chumita, who would later form team Chaindrive, were watching.

Bonneau, then 18, was the perfect demographic target for shows such as *Jackass.* He was young, tough, healthy, and, judging from the footage of him diving into trees from atop 18-wheelers and pancaking off of patio furniture in the *Full Leather Jacket* video, afraid of absolutely nothing.

Bonneau laughed at this observation, shrugging off his stunts as a response to simple boredom. "I watch a lot of *Jackass,* and I'd seen the Ruff Ryders video on MTV (where rapper DMX and a crew of New York riders wheelie and stoppie to a steamy, ghetto-rap backbeat) and shows like that, so when we were filming for our video, and things got dull, I'd just dream up some sick shit and do it," he said with a laugh. Being told he cannot accomplish something only goads Bonneau on to try it, regardless of the risk. He had only been riding two years when he caught sight of some particularly accomplished street extreme riders. He said that he knew from the first time he saw someone banging their needle off the rev limiter as they smoked a $150 rear Dunlop into shards that he had to get involved.

Involved is a great way to describe *Full Leather Jacket,* Chaindrive's first video release. It's one of the few stunt videos to combine the slapstick playfulness of the *Three Stooges* with some seriously on-edge motorcycle riding. Bonneau and Chumita were joined by former Universal Studios stuntman Holt in making the video, which basically proves in 30 minutes that street extreme riding is still testing uncharted waters and attracting new ideas. "I guess we just caught each other having fun and learning how to fall off our bikes," Bonneau said.

Chumita, 27, who was born in Youngstown, Ohio, had ridden motorcycles in one form or another since he was 19. The crew started out in loosely organized nighttime rides from an Orlando Hooters (as had LVX), eventually rid-

Chaindrive's first video release, *Full Leather Jacket,* is one of the few stunt videos to combine the slapstick playfulness of the Three Stooges with some seriously on-edge motorcycle riding.

Right: Camersport Photography

Wheelie Boy down. Jon Jon Buccheri's show-quality CBR Honda bites the dust after a routine stoppie turns violent.

ing home together to watch freestyle motocross videos, read European sportbike magazines, or just bounce new stunt ideas off each other, Chumita said. Chaindrive may have fun with improvised stunts and physical comedy, but Chumita said team leader Holt has always been a stickler for safety.

"You'll notice we never take off our helmets in our tape and I never take anything for granted. That's when you just might mess up. Even the simplest, sit-down wheelie could go wrong, so I really concentrate on what I'm doing. That's why I'm glad to be getting professional, paid shows, because on the street a group of guys may egg each other on to do crazier stunts, but after a while, somebody's gonna try it who isn't that skilled and then people get hurt," said Chumita, who performs stunts on a Suzuki GSX-R750 but has roadraced a Honda CBR F4 in the Formula USA CCS series at Roebling Road and Road Atlanta.

While Chumita was cutting apexes on the racing circuits, team leader Holt was playing to the crowds at Universal Studios Orlando theme park, recreating flashy stunts from Hollywood blockbusters three times daily.

Friendly and likable, Holt, 28, talks of his stunts—easily some of the sport's more incredible feats—with a matter-of-fact modesty. For instance, in their *Full Leather Jacket* video, he jumps rodeo-style from side to side off his roaring Kawasaki ZX-7 and, incredibly, rides underneath as a friend leaps in a split over his bike. In 1999's *Masters of Mayhem,* Holt can be seen dismounting a rolling seat-stand to somehow rescue a buddy's bike as it rolls along without Jamie Bridges, its fallen rider. "I saw him fall and thought, 'Oh great, his bike's gonna plow into me or hit somebody,' so I just steered over and grabbed the handlebar and put it to rest in the grass," he laughed.

Holt, who has been practicing his street extreme skills for eight hours each week since 1998, is intent on creating a new vibe in the sport, one where film-level entertainment can mix with ever more challenging stunts. Clips run in fast-motion, naked breasts flash, and sometimes it appears that Holt has as much fun getting stunts wrong as he does nailing them perfectly.

Clips run in fast-motion, naked breasts flash, and sometimes it appears that Holt has as much fun getting stunts wrong as he does nailing them perfectly.

Cy J. Cyr

Jon Jon Buccheri, his arm still bandaged from a recent hospital stay, shows off his battle citations for the day. Borrowing a friend's bike, he returned to compete in the games a day later.

"Living in Orlando, you'll see that everything down here is very television and entertainment-industry oriented, so it's only natural that when we make our videos we want them to have more than just motorcycle stunts—but they have to be entertaining and fun as well. If you don't dream up new tricks, people are going to fast-forward through your videos," said Holt, who stays true to his word by appearing in segments alternately spitting fire and dressing up as Eddie Murphy's 400-pound Grandma Klump in *Nutty Professor* for some funky disco moves. To skid behind his basically stock Kawasaki

ZX-7 at speeds up to 120 miles per hour, Holt opts not to wear metal skid-plates on his shoes. Instead, he wears policeman's duty boots and a pair of Fast Company's Kevlar-reinforced Draggin' Jeans for knee-down action.

"I'm not into freaking people out on the street, but when we found this deserted little piece of back road where we could drag knee and do it in our jeans, the looks on people's faces are just fantastic," Holt said. Although Chaindrive members practice incessantly, Bonneau is part of a whole new breed of motorcyclists that doesn't purchase motorcycles for transportation or travel, or to see the United States. Instead, they ride only for the thrill of the next stunt. "I started street riding just to learn stunts, and my first bike was a 1992 Kawasaki ZX-7. It was too damn big and heavy to stunt on but I got tired of watching the other guys doing it, so I just forced myself to learn as much as I could as quickly as I could," he said. A background in wakeboarding, skateboarding, motocross, and, in Bonneau's words, "just jumpin' off of shit whenever I felt like it," certainly helped.

Geographic locations and neighborhood affiliations mean little when **taut chains, nerves of steel, and 100-horsepower engines** can turn any street into a stunt show.

An East Coast Thang

While street extreme riders from the Southwest will tell you that long, straight roads are the best places to stunt, riders from all across the country have similar boasts to make about their home turf. But geographic locations and neighborhood affiliations mean little when taut chains, nerves of steel, and 100-horsepower engines can turn any street into a stunt show.

The intensity of traffic patterns and the always-available sidewalk crowds of big East Coast cities have provided some street extreme riders with an instant audience that's too ripe to resist. In 2000, Long Island, New York, stunt riders New York's Finest released a video depicting riders stunting amidst the neon of Times Square, while Pittsburgh's Knee-Draggin' Mafia (KDM) chose to blaze the tires in settings including gritty, drug-infested street corners and busy avenues—in full view of traffic.

Derrick "D-Mann" Daigle and Ronnie Giovelli discuss the finer points of motorcycling safety with Boston Heights Officer Joe Kraynik. "I swear, cops have a built-in wheelie sensor now," Giovelli complained.

Derrick "D-Mann" Daigle and Ricky "The Captain" Bookal create a modern moving pyramid with a pair of ATVs. Many stunt riders use the rugged off-road quad-runners to practice stunts that would easily destroy a streetbike.

Of course, this kind of riding continues to offer new dangers for its riders. KDM's Tim Andreas was practicing wheelies on his GSX-R1000 on a freeway outside of Pittsburgh when he noticed a state police helicopter hovering overhead. Passing the next two exits, he realized he'd been caught in the act, as state police cruisers were stationed to block the road. "I figured I was cold busted so I pulled over and was ready to give myself up," Andreas said. But the trooper just waved Andreas hurriedly away as if he couldn't be bothered. "Jesus Christ, kid, Vice President Al Gore's motorcade is about to pass through here and we're just keeping the roads clear," the trooper said.

Riding their streetfighter Honda CBR 600s, Rommel Dolabaille and Wyheem White of the stunt team the Jer-Z-Boyz admit a similarly narrow bent to their riding experiences. "I started out riding dirt bikes, and I got into streetbikes so I could do stunts. I tried riding to work, but you want to see something really dangerous, try riding rush hour on the New Jersey expressway. There's no stunt on earth as dangerous as that," said White, who can balance one of the sport's few sidesaddle stoppies.

Real love and dedication for street extreme: Reality Racing's Ronnie Giovelli sports leg tattoos, in addition to enough scar tissue to outfit a burn ward.

Jon Jon Buccheri and Paul Serpico, of Brooklyn's Wheelie Boyz, are part of an outstanding team that has startled shoppers and cops alike with a wicked set, including crossed-up vertical stoppies that hover nearly motionless and two-man wheelies of the highest order.

They share turf with the notoriously elusive Winky 1100, a big, bad Nubian in a chrome German army helmet who organizes annual outlaw stunt rides through Brooklyn. Andrew "Oildog" Empheresis, Winky's erstwhile mechanic and unofficial team leader, operates a custom sportbike shop in a dingy, graffiti-strewn section of Brooklyn, where he said stunt riding has become a mark of manhood for young bikers from all over New York's five boroughs.

Stunt riding has become a **mark of manhood** for young bikers from all over New York's five boroughs.

But even as Oildog Productions sells thousands of its strictly street videos, and promoters clamor to hire his crew for public appearances, Empheresis refuses to enter the professional stunt show circuit. "We're all about just keepin' it real up here in the streets. You get into letting people tell you how to do your thing or where to do it and pretty soon, all the fun is gone," he said.

According to twin brothers Peter and Paul Marmorato, of New York's Finest, the Big Apple is something of a street rider's paradise, mainly because of the city's notoriously tough reputation. "The cops usually don't even bother chasing after somebody just because we're pulling a wheelie or doing a rolling burnout past cars. There's too much real crime to deal with in New York," Peter said. "Yeah, they have more important things to worry about than us," Paul chimed in.

The Marmorato brothers, 29, started riding street extreme in 1998. Along with Steve Palumbo, New York's Finest are part of New York's huge, multiethnic street extreme movement, which they say encompasses thousands of riders ("but only a few really good ones," Paul joked) who trade challenges, stunts, and occasional bouts of road rash from New York's five boroughs to the freeways of New Jersey.

Paul said that on a typical Friday night on Coney Island, it's not unusual to find several dozen sportbike riders gathered around gas stations and restaurants, most of whom have practiced all week in hopes of busting that one move that will have the boys talking until the next weekend. "Ever since we first saw the Starboyz' tapes there was this sense of one-upmanship, this feeling of, 'Hey, if they can do that, why can't I?'" Peter said.

On a typical Friday night on Coney Island, it's not unusual to find **several dozen sportbike riders gathered** around gas stations and restaurants.

A midpractice break just days before a major stunt competition. The riders may face each other for prizes, but trade secrets and technical help are exchanged freely.

Todd Colbert may be pointing rearward, but he's clearly looking toward the future with the formation of the World Stunt Riding Championships, his new competitive series for amateur and professional stunt riders.

Riding an assortment of road-weary machines, including a dazzlingly hokey GSX-R1000 wrapped entirely in aluminum foil and a fully customized Yamaha quad-runner, New York's Finest are typical of East Coast street extreme teams, who utilize just about any vehicle they can. Although ATVs were designed to basically serve as rural delivery vehicles or to provide transportation over rough, wooded terrain, several street extreme riders have flipped that countrified role and reinvented the quad as a new urban status symbol, much in the same way that hip-hoppers have reassigned Timberland all-terrain boots and Tommy Hilfiger's outdoor wear.

In the Starboyz' *FTP 2* video, riders perform wheelie quads through a suburban housing plan while chatting on their cell phones. Some absolutely unbelievable quads, replete with running lights, $4,000 paint jobs, and full Ohlins suspension systems are not uncommon at Brooklyn stunt rallies, said Paul Marmorato, of New York's Finest. "As long as it stunts, we'll try it, because people get bored easily and they always want to see something new," Peter said.

"Quads are really cool because they bounce back well and because they're geared really low and have lots of torque just off idle. They're perfect for practicing stunts. Plus, they don't tend to get as banged-up as the streetbikes do, so lots of guys really like to have them around," explained Daigle, who is nearly as adept on four-wheelers as he is on two.

One of the finest examples of the quad-runner's ability to impart lessons in throttle control to streetbike riders was revealed in the practice sessions before the Starboyz' Stunt Festival at Cleveland's Thompson Dragway in August 2001.

A daylong open-track practice saw 30 or so of the most talented street extreme riders from across the country honing their skills and alternately trying to impress each other along the crowded quarter-mile, with varying degrees of success. There was a series of stunning, two-up wheelies from newcomers Jason Williams and Patti Perkins, of Fort Lauderdale, Florida's, Broward Boyz, and Buccheri, of Brooklyn's Wheelie Boyz, who unexpectedly lost control of a very routine-looking stoppie, all but destroying his beautifully restored 1998 Honda CBR 900— and his wrist—in the process.

And then, out of the smoke from a dozen simultaneous burnouts came the dull grind of a quad-runner's small-bore motor. Lying across the seat and clutching the handlebars backward was a wild, dreadlocked ragamuffin, dressed only in jeans and tie-dyed T-shirt.

"Who is this guy?" everybody seemed to say out loud at once.

"Hey, what's up, mon?" he said and introduced himself as Rob Marley, son of late reggae superstar Bob Marley. Marley, 29, is a featured rider in the Miami Warriors, a well-known stunt crew where each rider is responsible for customizing a Yamaha R-1 in a highly personalized design.

As if Marley's reverse Christ On A Quad weren't enough, he shifted and swayed through the track full of riders by piloting his Yamaha YZF-R1 in a full tank-stand. Marley then returned down the strip draped across the motorcycle's seat sideways, seemingly steering the bike through sheer intuition.

Comprised mainly of recent immigrants from Jamaica, the 50-member Warriors are part stunt team, part social scene, and part customizing circle. The team's unofficial spokesman is Ricky "The Captain" Bookal, 36. He said Miami has been relatively slow to catch on to the street extreme movement, but teams such as The Zoo Crew, which favors fur-covered R1 Yamahas, have recently begun staging stunt festivals throughout South Florida. The Warriors started out back in 1989, mainly as a crew of guys who got together to share and compare customizing tricks on their R1s.

From there, Bookal said, stunting came about as an added attraction for the crowds that seemed to gather whenever they went for a ride.

In early 2001, England's *Streetfighters* magazine ran a profile story about the Warriors, a story that focused more on the world-class custom bikes than the stunt prowess of Marley and crew. But with a full-length video on the way, the group's skills will soon get their due.

Zen-like and quiet, Marley offered little in the way of details about his unusual but clearly devastating technique.

Zen-like and quiet, Marley offered little in the way of details about his unusual but clearly devastating technique. However, Warrior Sli, whose 1999 R1 is decorated with cryptic, glow-in-the-dark computer-chip graphics, offered a little insight. "He just does his own thing and does it his own

way. I'm not really sure he knows how his balance became so good, but he never seems to fall. Not ever," Sli said.

Marley, who carries the family's gift for music and works part-time as a singer and songwriter, attributes his childhood in Kingston, Jamaica, with teaching him the ins and outs of fast street riding. "There are laws over in Jamaica against bikers riding anything larger than a 600 on the streets because the cops' cars aren't fast enough to catch a really big bike. Well, there was always somebody trying to find a way around that one by bringing in big bikes and just putting 600 decals on them, or faking the paperwork," he said.

Kids being kids, Marley said he and his sportbike-mounted friends would routinely test their Honda CBR600s and Kawasaki ZX-6Rs against the fastest police cruisers on the island. "You either learned to ride good and ride fast, or you'd end up losing your bike," he said. When the street extreme movement made its way south in the late 1990s, Marley said turning his hard-won street skills into stunts was much easier than he expected. "It just came to me naturally, and I started doing it just to relax," he said with a shrug.

Savage, another dreadlocked Miami Warriors member who got his start riding in Jamaica, views the street extreme phenomenon philosophically—as though it is a social movement that is unique to motorcycling for its ability to bring disparate groups of people together.

A scene from an upcoming Knee Draggin' Mafia video: Like most street extreme tapes, this one started out as a collection of crash footage and weekend fun.

Savage views the street extreme phenomenon philosophically—as though it is **a social movement** that is unique to motorcycling for its ability to bring disparate groups of people together.

"You look around you and you see all types of people—black, white, male, female—and they're all getting along great and having fun with this. That's one thing that sportbikes and stunt riding do that you don't see other places—it brings all sorts of people together," he said.

Midwest Madness

Large, well-organized stunt shows are slow in coming in the Midwest, where literally dozens of stunt teams have sprung up in recent years. Just outside of Chicago, the Loose Cannons (L.C.) formed its own street extreme team in 1999, one of the Midwest's first. The team's unofficial leader, Jamie "Superman" Cotner, 30, credits the endless Illinois straightaways for helping create his legendary long-distance wheelies. When he first bought a Yamaha YZF-R1, Cotner, who is married and started stunting in 1998 after watching videos in local bike shops, pulled a wheelie for 3.5 miles, reaching 145 miles per hour in the process. Cotner had several years of street riding under his belt and figured this to be a fairly tough act to follow. And it was, but not for long. "I started meeting kids every weekend who had just started riding but were some pretty stylin' stunt riders. We started hanging out and the next thing you know, we've got the Loose Cannons," he explained.

Among L.C.'s varying roster of riders is Chip McPheeters, a 26-year-old former college linebacker skilled at muscling stunts out of a bike as though he's teaching the motorcycle a lesson, and Greg Walsh, the team's resident freestyle stunt expert, adept at flamingo wheelies—from the passenger pegs, no less. Enough newcomers have surfaced in recent years that the L.C.'s video, *Wheelies 'N Stuff,* features a bigger cast than Cecil B. DeMille's *The Ten Commandments.* Cotner is pleased to see the growth in a sport where, not so long ago, he felt terribly alone. "When I first started, I was out doing stunts and stuff in traffic and the cops were staking my house out and I remember wondering, does anybody else out here know about this?"

Cy J. Cyr

In rural Wisconsin, twenty-somethings Dan Urban and Cory Kufahl were wondering the same thing. The two were riding wheelies and burnouts without ever having met each other. Both guys had their faithful followings of local sportbike riders, and, eventually, as with the two fastest gunslingers in an old Western, the two passed each other by accident.

"Every time we'd go past each other, we'd do wheelies and see who could outdo each other. We finally met and we started talking and decided to get together and do some filming," said Urban. They formed the D-Aces, one of the Midwest's best-known street extreme teams.

Urban credits his years spent riding BMX bicycles and racing amateur motocross with helping his street skills. By far, he and others agree that motocross skills—learning how to drop, slide, and brake hard on a bike—make for more controlled street extreme.

By far, most agree that motocross skills—learning how to drop, slide, and brake hard on a bike—make for more controlled street extreme.

Moving off the streets into the performance arena, the D-Aces are among the few U.S. street teams to perform outside home soil, with a show in Guatemala City. According to Urban, a vibrant sportbike and roadracing scene is happening in Central America, but with streetbikes so expensive south of the border, few riders would venture to stunt on such cherished possessions. "These guys all ride really hard down in El Salvador and Guatemala, but I don't think they'd ever seen a rolling stoppie done from about 60 miles per hour. They were so impressed they were losing their minds," he said.

The D-Aces are also notable for working their skills dressed in full-leather racing suits, a rarity in this country. That's because as the movement has spread, an unofficial dress code has emerged that's almost universally adhered to among street extreme afi-

Camerasport Photography

cionados. The audience at the 2001 Starboyz Cleveland Stunt Festival, for instance, resembled a convention of fake fur salesmen. And just try to find a New York City stunt rider who isn't wearing Scott motocross goggles and a chromed German army helmet, though these riders dismiss full-race leathers as too restrictive for fluid body movement.

Kevin Calo of New Jersey's Loose Riders celebrates his stunning second-place finish. The Loose Riders combine hip-hop style with inner-city cool, performing to a gangsta rap background.

The road to enlightenment is strewn with broken bones. Here, Rev. Paul Sinclair, of London, forgets why Gary Rothwell insisted that he hold on tight during a wheelie launch. In the coming months, Sinclair would suffer far worse as he rode stunts on his Honda Fireblade and Suzuki Bandit 1200.

Tea with Your Wheelie?

Overseas, things are different. Whether out on the streets or in the established, big-business arena of European and British stunt riding, full-race leathers are the norm for sportbike riders. But the European stunt scene differs from street extreme in more ways than just fashion. Such well-known riders as Jimmy Fireblade, Doug Coates, and A. C. Farias compete in well-attended, sanctioned events that are far removed from the free-for-all atmosphere of American street extreme. At the Scottish Motorcycle Show and the Annual European Stunt Bike Championships, stunt riders are judged by a panel of professional commentators for distance, originality, and style, said Howard Cartiledge, stunt coordinator and associate editor of Britain's popular *Streetfighters* magazine.

> Overseas, things are different. **The European stunt scene differs from street extreme in more ways than just fashion.**

"Our stunt festivals have been going on since the 1980s, and when we see videos of the Yanks doing stunts in traffic and on the highways, it's an incredible sight, but I don't think that's quite the image we're after," Cartiledge said with typical British aplomb.

While British stunt riding enjoys a higher level of visibility and overall acceptability than its American counterpart, few U.S. teams are desperate to imitate what they've seen in popular European stunt videos. Urban and Kufahl, however, are great admirers of the riding

For Rev. Paul Sinclair, stunt riding is akin to virtual gospel. His bike? A zebra-striped Yamaha R1.

Self-professed originator of street extreme and Las Vegas Extreme member Pauly Sherer shows why his sometimes grandoise claims are backed up by unparalleled talent. An exercise in balance and balls, Sherer's Leap of Faith is one of the toughest stunts around. *Nick O'Brien*

Cy J. Cyr

and fashion styles of the Brits. They said the one-piece leathers send a good message of safety to audiences, which helps to attract sponsors who are otherwise turned off by street extreme's lackadaisical attitudes toward safety.

However, that saw cuts both ways. For instance, living in London hasn't prevented the gospel of American-style street extreme riding from spreading. And for Rev. Paul Sinclair, stunt riding is akin to virtual gospel. Vicar of the Church of the High Road in Willisden, Sinclair, 36, is a cheerful Phil Collins look-alike. He's ridden motorbikes most of his life, even serving a stint as one of London's fabled despatch, or motorcycle messenger riders. Surviving several years of riding through the suicidal, left-side traffic of the British capital was nothing compared to assuming his post at Willisden's church, Sinclair said.

His community is composed mainly of new Jamaican immigrants, and with its decaying housing stock and rampant drug crimes, Willisden is one of the few British communities to have witnessed drive-by shootings. Sinclair, who operates under the name the Faster Pastor, was not intimidated by Willisden, even after he was beaten unconscious by a gang of youths after first arriving. A spirited rider of his Honda CBR 900 Fireblade, Sinclair started whipping up stoppies and wheelies in and around his parish. These were skills that gained Sinclair a level of admiration from some of the neighborhood's toughest gangsters.

In time, Sinclair contacted Brit stunt legend Gary Rothwell to perform a charity event for the Willisden church, which was covered by the press on both sides of the Atlantic. In 2000, Sinclair had somehow located a copy of the Starboyz' *FTP* video, which he studied until the VCR nearly ate his tape, he said. It didn't matter. By then, London's Faster Pastor was well on his way to becoming Britain's best-known street extreme rider.

Sinclair was captured by the BBC for a segment on Europe's multifaceted motorcycle subcultures, performing a series of balls-out kneedowns around a busy traffic roundabout. His bike? A zebra-striped, furred-out Yamaha R1. In the end, Sinclair was no different from street extreme riders everywhere. They tend to share a central belief, that, even if they couldn't make a few bucks from selling homemade videos, and even if nobody was watching, they'd still be out there risking it all for the thrill of a perfectly rolled stoppie or a burnout through all six gears.

"I consider all of us pretty lucky to ride our motorcycles and have people actually care. That's all we'd be doing even if we didn't have the fans," said LVX's Sherer. He's never been more right.

Getting one's knee down while circumventing a traffic roundabout is the British stunt scene's signature move. Diesel spills and cross-traffic always make this stunt a dangerous challenge. *Nick O'Brien*

For Fun or Profit?

Bringing motorcycle stunt riders together for fun or for profit has become a much more common concern during recent years. While nearly all riders agree that their sport could use a boost from mainstream media and inclusion in ESPN's X Games or NBC's Gravity Games to help galvanize street extreme in the public eye, initial attempts to organize riders under a central banner have proven difficult.

The XSBA held its first annual stunt competition during the Formula USA roadraces at Pennsylvania's Pocono International Raceway in August 2001, but many of the headlining riders decided not to attend. Chief organizer Cliff Nobles, brother of veteran roadracer Tripp Nobles, still enjoyed a full roster of talent at the show—testimony to the size of the streetbike extreme movement—including New Jersey's Loose Riders, LVX, and the D-Aces, among others. Though it was hard to imagine street extreme riders on a racetrack, the professionally judged competition drew tremendous audience response from the 14,000 roadracing spectators.

Though some notable riders balked at signing on with the XSBA in its early stages, shows such as these clearly offer new outlets for two-wheeled creativity.

Though some notable riders balked at signing on with the XSBA in its early stages—mainly out of fear that mainstream organization of their sport will only dilute it and benefit corporate promoters and not rank-and-file stunt riders—shows such as these clearly offer new outlets for two-wheeled creativity. "I'm all for getting kids off the streets and into safe environments to ride stunts, but when we get invited to a stunt show that none of us had a hand in creating or organizing, I don't know whether I want any part of it," Peter Marmorato, of New York's Finest, said.

Daigle and Colbert, of Team X-Treem, hope to someday coalesce all of the country's stunt shows into a central staging body; but many other street extreme riders are reluctant to lend their services to the roadracing world, which they view as an uptight, rules-laden antithesis to what they do.

"You'll notice that here, and in the X Games, you don't see some fat, old dudes with whistles hanging around their necks yelling at people, telling us we screwed up or did some stunt the wrong way. That's what I hated about road racing: Your bike has to be just right for some bullshit tech inspection or you can get disqualified for the slightest little bit of doing something wrong. This is at least something we can do for ourselves and we don't have to ask anybody's permission to do it," said Starboy Marino.

This open resentment toward any involvement by such corporate promoters as SFX/Clear Channel Media is typical of extreme athletes. During the 2001 Summer X Games in Philadelphia, several prominent skateboarders and BMX riders declined to participate in the competition, dismissing the X Games as a corporate sellout. That the event staged skateboarding competitions in arenas built at the Philadelphia County Courthouse—the exact site where numerous local skateboarders had been arrested and fined for public skating in years past—was not lost on the faithful.

"When in doubt, run!" That was Kawasaki Ninja rider and wheelie merchant James Johnson's motto. One who bragged about being "10–1 in police chases," in early 2000 Johnson fled from police after being spotted popping a wheelie in traffic. After four miles, police broke off the pursuit, where speeds reached 140 miles per hour. Sadly, Johnson was killed instantly when he failed to negotiate a turn and ran into a stand of trees. His helmet encapsulates the irony of how his life ended.
Steven Adams

Chapter 4

The Skillz
To Pay the Bills

Riders usually learn how to perform and execute stunts as a result of oral or visual experiences. In other words, riders usually create new stunts from watching others or simply invent new moves from their imagination. Sometimes this works. Very often, as evidenced by the frequent appearance of cracked motorcycle side panels and bandaged arms and legs, it doesn't.

Holt, who seems as fearless as a cracked-out trapeze artist, has struggled for months to perfect a move he calls the Switchback Decompression, which involves sitting backward on his Kawasaki ZX-7 Ninja and then whipping his legs and torso around into a seat-mounted handstand. From there, Holt flips over backward in a full, 70-mile-per-hour somersault to land on his feet, where he skis behind the riderless bike.

Several early attempts were successful. But then, during a practice session, Holt hyperextended his right knee, ending that stunt's progress for at least a few months. But Holt will not be surprised if he sees the Switchback Decompression resurface before he's healed up and back on the streets, for dozens of riders watched him practice the maneuver. Somewhere, there's a rider working overtime to nail down the Switchback Decompression and perhaps improve on it as well.

Stunt rider Jamie "Superman" Cotner, of Chicago's Loose Cannons, is typical of stunt riders whose expertise is partly self-taught from watching videos, and partly derived from group lessons that spring up whenever more than one street extreme rider gets together in a single location. "There may be a stunt, like the flying wheelie, that you've been trying to perfect for months that you just can't get right. Then, you'll meet somebody who's got it right and you end up working it and talking things back and forth while you practice, and the next thing you know, it's part of your routine," he said.

Savage, a rider with the Miami Warriors, is another stunt rider who has relied heavily on the generosity of the street extreme community to perfect

Cover art from the Knee-Draggin' Mafia's (KDM) With A Vengeance video. Zoot suits and rolling burnouts are always in style. Left to right (standing) are the Pittsburgh clan's members: Ray McClelland, Mark Hauger, Mark Mradvich, and Glenn Wells. Seated is KDM's Tim Andreas.

stunts he's seen in videos and on the streets. "The coolest thing is, people don't really care if you try one of their stunts. They see it as a compliment when you're out there trying to do a move they invented," he observed. In most cases, newcomers will manage to improve or alter a stunt in some way, either through a subtle nuance or body position or with a wild flourish of style. Consider the way the basic stoppie has evolved into Colbert's rotating, 180-degree Sidewinder version; Holt's bizarre, left-handed variation; or the Jer-Z-Boyz' shocking-to-see sidesaddle maneuver.

In most cases, newcomers will manage to improve or alter a stunt in some way, either through a subtle nuance or body position, or with a wild flourish of style.

There's more debate over exactly who was responsible for originating the principal moves of stunt riding, although Daigle is as believable as anyone when he claims to have "sat on a roadside in Las Vegas a few years ago, trying out new stunts," and then straining his brain to think up names for them. "Today, when I go somewhere and some kid tells me, 'He just did a Switchback Insane,' I think, damn, that was my move from a few years ago. In a way, it makes you feel proud," he said.

Regardless of their origins, the constant experimentation and need to one-up the next guy means that street extreme's repertoire of stunts is not in any danger of running dry anytime soon. Following are a few of the experts discussing the how and why of their favorite moves.

Team: Starboyz

Arguably one of the longest-running teams in street extreme, Ohio's Starboyz have ridden at the front of the pack for over five years. From ghetto-fabulous inner-city street antics and five-mile freeway wheelies to major, mainstream exposure on cable television's Speedvision network and just about every British bad-boy sportbike magazine in existence, the Starboyz have taken fake fur to places Zsa Zsa Gabor never dreamed existed.

Videos: *FTP 1, FTP 2, Road Rage, Foggy Meets The Starboyz* (U.K. release), and *FTP 2 $^1/_2$,* with *FTP 3* scheduled to be released by the time of this book's publication.

The Starboyz have taken fake fur to places Zsa Zsa Gabor never dreamed existed.

Planted firmly on his head at 70 miles per hour, J. T. Holt extends his legs, a bizarre sight that usually ends up sending the competition home disheartened.

RIDER: SCOTT CARABOOLAD

Bike: *Honda CBR900* Fur upholstery, leaky radiator, concave gas tank, 16-inch front wheel.

Favorite Stunt: "It's funny, but I thought I'd really get off on the skating-be-hind-the-bike stuff like Gary Rothwell does, but I cut out a pair of metal soles and tried it around a parking lot, and after about 100 feet I stopped the bike and thought, 'Well, this is pretty weak.' Since then, the skills I've been working on the most are the slow-speed, crawling vertical wheelies."

"The skills I've been working on the most are the slow-speed, crawling vertical wheelies." —Scott Caraboolad, Starboyz

"Kevin Marino and I put skid plates on the backs of our bikes because they let up this wild shower of sparks if you hit it just right and drag it. But you can see where this has ground off the end of my exhaust can and the taillight—well, just forget it. The secret is to drop down into first gear and as the front end comes up like it's going over, past the flip-point, start applying the rear brake with a whole lot of force to slow the whole thing down. Too much brake and the front end comes slamming down hard enough that the bars will shake right out of your hands; not enough brake and it's just a sort of slow, lame wheelie. It's a really wild sight and it takes a lot of arm strength to balance it just right, but it's worth it because it takes like five minutes from the time people notice you until you're past them, and they're like, 'How can he ride a wheelie that slow?'"

RIDER: KEVIN MARINO

Bike: *GSX-R750* Leopard fur, Two Brothers exhaust, actually gets cleaned regularly.

Favorite Stunt: "Anything I do that gets people more charged up is going to get me all hyped so I perform better, but my favorite has got to be a long, long stoppie. People are always asking how you get a stoppie to roll forward and they think it's all about just jamming on the brakes real hard. You have to get up some good speed—get rolling at about 50 or 60—and shift your body weight up onto the gas tank. Then lock up the front brake. You can tell when you have just the right amount of pressure—the back end will start to drift up just before the wheel locks up. If you get your balance to the right point just over the front axle, you can drift them [the stoppies] forever."

> "Anything I do that gets people more **charged up is going to get me all hyped** so I perform better." —*Kevin Marino, Starboyz*

RIDER: "BIG DAVE" SONSKY

This part-time Starboy and freelance rider has shared the road with everyone from New York's Finest to the test pilots at England's *Super-Bike* magazine.

Bike: *1998 Honda CBR900* Mismatched wheels featuring various flat-spots, tiger-striped fur, Two Brothers exhaust, and altered sprocket gearing.

Favorite Stunt: "It would have to be the vertical wheelie sitting on the bars. Any long, stand-up wheelie is great because it gets harder and harder the longer you try to hold it. Always in second gear, I just grab the handlebars and pull up. Because we run different gearing on the front and the rear sprockets, the bike will come up high without even having to use the clutch. That's why people are always asking, 'How do you guys pull such smooth stand-ups in your videos?' Well, it's all in the gearing. At first, it seems weird being up that high, and the looks on people's faces are unbelievable, but it's cool to see truckers who'll give you a big blast on the air horn, and some guys in cars really love it, too."

Savage, a Miami Warrior, shows off a short, powerburst wheelie. "You don't need any clutch for this. It's all throttle in first gear if your bike's powerful enough. It's just something quick that we do on the street to show a little skill."

Team: Miami Warriors

Up from the sultry, sunny islands of Jamaica to the mean streets of Miami come the Warriors, an all-Yamaha R1–mounted crew of custom sportbike wizards and street extreme experts. Crowds often don't know whether to trip out on the $25,000 tricked-out Yamahas, which feature glow-in-the-dark paint jobs and futuristic electronic surveillance systems, or the Warriors' mad-crazy approach to stunt riding. Whether using dirt bikes or quad-runners, the Warriors are destined to become Miami's hottest visual attraction this side of a South Beach thong contest.

Crowds often don't know whether to trip out on the $25,000 tricked-out Yamahas or on the Warriors' mad-crazy approach to stunt riding.

Zen and the art of motorcycle stunt riding: Rob Marley and his decidedly cool, calm approach to street extreme shows how mind control equals body control.

RIDER: ROB MARLEY

Bike: *2000 Yamaha YZF-R1* Custom-cut Wave brake rotors, custom paint, Hindle full exhaust system, Tobey steering damper, dual rearview video cameras.

Favorite Stunt: "You name it," quipped Marley. Blessed with an uncanny sense of balance, Marley is one of the few street extreme riders capable of actually steering his motorcycle while standing on the gas tank. Slow and steady rather than furiously fast, Marley is all about balance and control. He's also adept at something called the Christ On A Quad, which involves mounting a quad while parked and then cracking the throttle and leaning his body weight forward in one smooth movement, which brings the machine up into a full-standing vertical wheelie. And this is just part of Marley's warm-up, he said. "One of the best things I like to do is short handstands on my gas tanks. It takes all of my wrist strength to sort of do a push-up onto the gas tank, and from there, I shoot my legs out behind me fully extended so that, from the front or from the sides, it really looks like I'm almost levitating over the length of the motorcycle. I've been working on steering the bike like that, which only involves shifting the weight across my shoulders. I like to lie across the seat and steer by dipping my head or my legs, too, and that's something people on the street really go crazy for," he said.

> **"One of the best things I like to do is** short handstands on my gas tanks. It really looks **like I'm almost levitating over the length of the** motorcycle." —Rob Marley, Miami Warriors

Team: Chaindrive

Like a cross between MTV's *Jackass* and a Hollywood stuntman school, Chaindrive is exceptional not only for doing knee-downs on public roads, but for being canny enough to find an actual curved piece of road in Florida. They've also figured out how to ride, standing on the gas tank while twirling nunchakus and on grass no less; how to breathe fire after a rolling stoppie; and, best of all, remain cool while doing so in a part of Florida where 4-inch cockroaches are known to splatter across a helmet face-shield!

Videos: *Full Leather Jacket, Urban Assault, Moving Violation*

RIDER: J. T. HOLT

Bike: Kawasaki *ZX-7R* All stock except for crash protectors and steering stabilizer.

Favorite Stunt: "The Switchback Insane is my favorite stunt and I swear, last year *I* invented this one. It's pretty much like what they do on horseback at the rodeo, where a rider will go from a handstand into a headstand on the saddle. I wait until the balance really feels just perfect and then I drop onto my head and fully extend my arms and legs. People say it looks really weird,

Adam Chumita

Adam Chumita

The La-Z-Boy Switchback, a patently silly move first seen in the *Las Vegas Extremes* video and now a favorite of Chaindrive and Adam Chumita. "I look relaxed, but it's a little weird not knowing what's coming up in front of you," said Holt.

and when you're rolling along upside down looking off the rear of the bike, it feels weird, too. It took maybe a couple of weeks to get it right, but the hardest part was getting comfortable and learning how to flip back over and get my legs behind the handlebars so I don't lose control. You have to do this move really fast because that balance point where you can stand on your head while the bike has the throttle locked on doesn't last that long before the wind starts hitting your legs. I recently started working on the Reverse Switchback Decompression Insane, where I pretty much do the Switchback Insane and then flip off of the back of the bike, grab the handrail, and go into a ski mode, where I trail behind the bike for a few blocks."

RIDER: ADAM CHUMITA

Bike: *Suzuki GSX-R750* Akropovic full-exhaust system, custom paint, cracked windshield.

Favorite Stunt: "By far my favorite stunt is the Reverse Tank Stand, which I do in *Full Leather Jacket.* That one really scares people because from a distance, they see this guy standing on his motorcycle, but then when they get closer, they realize that I'm looking in the other direction. The twist-off from the front-facing position while on the tank is the hardest part, but the secret is just turning the idle adjustment screw up far enough that the bike keeps running while your hands are off the bars—that, and not upsetting the bike when you jump up and switch around. After I was comfortable doing that, I invented a new one I call the Rodeo. Basically, I do a switchback while in the seat and hop over the front fairing and sit with my butt over the headlights, facing backward while I'm moving at about 60 miles per hour. My legs are pointed over the handlebars and I sit with my arms folded. It may seem hard to believe, but I'm actually comfortable riding backward. As long as the front end is in good shape and you don't get any wobbles or end up smacking into the handlebars with your legs while turning around, it's not that scary. We tried this one at first by trying to get off the front of the bike and skiing by being pushed along by the bike but that just wasn't gonna work. Not yet, anyway."

"By far my favorite stunt is the Reverse Tank Stand, which I do in Full Leather Jacket. That one really scares people." — *Adam Chumita, Chaindrive*

Dan Urban of Wisconsin's D-Aces shows how to pull a circular burnout without ever getting in the saddle. Some riders have started spelling their names and drawing pictures with the black rubber tire marks.

Team: D-Aces

Out in the flat, broad plains of America's Dairyland (honest—that's what the Wisconsin license plates said!), the D-Aces have a reputation for performing high-flying street extreme stunts. The Suzuki-mounted team has some of the most durable and well-used stuntbikes on the circuit and features more and fancier braces than you'd see at a high school dance. D-Aces team members earned their stripes by defying gravity and international traffic laws, and by staging the first-ever motorcycle stunt shows in Guatemala. After conquering the Southern hemisphere on one wheel, the D-Aces plan to stoppie over a Holstein cow sometime in the near future.

D-Aces team members earned their stripes by defying gravity and international traffic laws, and by staging the first-ever motorcycle stunt shows in Guatemala.

Videos: Set It Off

RIDER: DAN URBAN

Bike: *Suzuki GSX-R750 GSX-R600 motor, missing windshield, concave gas tank.*

Favorite Stunt: "I guess my favorite stunts are any with my legs draped over the windshield—I don't care if it's wheelies or stoppies or rolling burnouts. They're all fun. The funny thing about doing the legs-up thing is learning how to safely get your body twisted around and up there. It looks really easy, but sitting on the handlebars, you have to be real careful not to upset the handlebars when you move at first from the seat, to the gas tank, and then to the bars themselves—all while you're rolling along.

"Nothing gets the crowds crazy like a long, tire-bursting burnout, though. I did one at the Pocono Stunt Festival and people loved it. What you basically do is hold on the brake and let the clutch out as you rev the throttle in gear. It's really tricky to start rolling because you have to hold a little bit of tension on the front brake so the bike doesn't just grab traction and take off. But you also have to let off the brake enough that the bike slowly rolls forward. Then, while you're doing all of this, you have to work through the gears so you don't hit the rev limiter too fast. Then the tire will actually burn and make a ton of smoke, but you're not really taking off as much tread as if you were doing a stationary burnout. If you can stop and make the tire explode with a real, real long wail on the throttle at the end, that's the bomb."

"My favorite stunts are any with my legs draped over the windshield—I don't care if it's wheelies or stoppies or rolling burnouts." —Dan Urban, D-Aces

Jon Jon Buccheri would not reveal how he manages to drop into a rolling skid-burnout while his feet are miles away from the rear brake pedal. "I'm not giving this one up. Figure it out for yourselves."

RIDER: CORY KUFAHL

Bike: *Suzuki TL1000S* Concave gas tank for tank wheelies, extra frame bracing, full Hindle exhaust system.

Favorite Stunt: "My favorite stunt is the high-speed stoppie. The TL has such great torque that even in a tight space, you can get up enough quick speed to really crank it up when you get on the brakes. Having the strength to hold the bike up once it's nosed over is a big part of the control, and because I work out with weights a lot (that's an understatement: Kufahl is a competitive bodybuilder), I can practice holding it up for a long time."

Team: Wheelie Boyz

Brooklyn's Wheelie Boyz is a loose-knit collection of riders from the Brooklyn area, a neighborhood known for hard-riding sportbikers. Jon Jon Buccheri, who rides a chromed-out and well-maintained Honda CBR900RR, is a jack-of-all-trades when it comes to stunt riding: Ask him for a favorite stunt, and he's off in a blur of spent rubber and exhaust gases, running through his full routine of mind-bending stunts. "I watch the videos and I can do pretty much anything that's going on. It's just a matter of practice," he said.

> **Brooklyn's Wheelie Boyz is a loose-knit collection of riders from the Brooklyn area, a neighborhood known for hard-riding sportbikers.**

VIDEOS: THOUGHT U KNEW
RIDER: JON JON BUCCHERI

Bike: *1998 Honda CBR900* Buccheri favors a clean, customized mount, an anomaly among riders who seem to enjoy bashing up their bikes as much as stunting them.

Favorite Stunt: Custom bike and all, Buccheri is not afraid to take chances. His vertical, slow-crawl wheelies are smoother than most, which Buccheri attributes to having changed the sprocket gearing on his bike, along with years of perfecting smooth throttle control.

"I think the tough part is you can't see what's up ahead. The whole bike is straight up and if you hold it too long, you can hear the motor start running rough because it's starving the top end of oil. You have to know just how long you can ride one." Likewise, his one-handed stoppies, both from the seat and from the handlebars, are scary-low. "You actually get a better feel for how far over the bike's going when you're sitting on the bars. Your feet are real close to the ground, so if you tip too far and have to jump off in a hurry, you're right there. Your only worry, I guess, is getting run over by the bike."

RIDER: PAUL SERPICO

Bike: 1998 Honda CBR900

Favorite Stunt: "I love to bust a massive, vertical stoppie. There's nothing else that makes people scream and makes people think you're about to lose it like a stoppie. The key is you gotta get some decent speed up if you really want to loft the back end. The bike needs to be going at least about 35, 45 miles per hour and then when you get ready to grab the front brake, you shift your weight way forward up around the tank, which helps put weight over the front wheel. After a while, we got so we could hold the brake frozen and hold the bike up for, like, a few seconds' hang time. It looks like you're just frozen and it may go either way," he said.

Joe Frazier reminds himself of the cardinal rule of rolling burnouts: Too much juice gets you loose.

Paul Serpico of New York's Wheelie Boyz provides ballast for a two-up endo.

Team: Team X-Treem

Todd Colbert's Team X-Treem works like an all-star collection of street extreme's best-known riders. Based in Florida, where Colbert spends his days practicing his moves on an airport runway, Team X-Treem has performed with J. T. Holt, Jason Britton, Jorge Arana, and Lori Colbert. Some of their signature moves include a Four-Man Christ and

high-speed pavement skiing. The granddaddy of the stunt movement, who, along with Daigle, is responsible for what is easily the movement's most extreme stunt, the vaunted Ghost Ride, is currently moving into the promotions arena, staging national stunt riding competitions and producing videos of up-and-coming riders.

Videos: *Team X-Treem, Masters of Mayhem, Moving Violation, Road Rage, Judgment Day*

> Team X-Treem works like an all-star collection of street extreme's best-known riders.

RIDER: TODD COLBERT

Bike: *Suzuki GSX-R1100* Streetfighter with Renthal motocross handlebars, custom paint, Vortec exhaust, WP steering damper.

Favorite Stunt: "My favorite stunt is a 180-degree Sidewinder Stoppie, twisting all the way around and landing and coming into a wheelie. I've called it the whippet, and it took a few months to learn because if you don't get it just right, you dump it right on the ground.

"The whole stoppie thing is kind of unnatural because I remember the first time I pulled a stoppie, and it felt like I was just gonna fly right over the handlebars. It's definitely something you have to get used to. The Ghost Ride that D-Mann and I came up with at the airstrip took a really long time to get right. We had practiced it as much as we could and when we were ready, we brought out a helicopter to film it for *Moving Violation*. It came off a lot better than we'd expected. The hard part, which you can see in the videotape, comes when I'm riding D-Mann on the front of my bike and his bike is just rolling down the asphalt with nobody on it. I had to catch up to his bike and get him to drift back on it, but since my sight lines were so limited with him on the front of the bike, it's really hard to see where I'm going. We got it right and we got it on film, and that's what mattered."

> "My favorite stunt is a 180-degree Sidewinder Stoppie, twisting all the way around and landing and coming into a wheelie."
> *—Todd Colbert, Team X-Treem*

RIDER: DERRICK "D–MANN" DAIGLE

Bike: *Suzuki GSX-R1000.*

Favorite Stunt: "Because I used to race Jet Skis, I learned pretty early on that not upsetting the handlebars is very important. Once you learn that, you can pretty much learn a whole bunch of different stunts, from the Switchback Insane to all sorts of handstands.

"We started doing the fender-grab wheelie because after riding really long wheelies, we just saw that big ol' front wheel staring at us and I thought, 'I wonder if I can reach out and grab the fender?' The answer is yes, but it's really tricky because as you lean forward to reach for the fender, you put weight over the front wheel, which tends to make it come back down. The skiing thing is hard because you can't upset the bike while sliding back over the seat hump, but once your feet are on the ground, you have to just sort of find your pressure point and not stand on your feet too hard and create too much friction. You have to be just light enough on your feet to keep them skating."

Team: Las Vegas Extremes

One of the first and biggest U.S. stunt teams, Las Vegas Extremes emerged at roughly the same time as the Starboyz, but with vastly different approaches to

After watching a rider fall from his bike only to see the motorcycle continue rolling forward, Todd Colbert and Derrick "D-Mann" Daigle decided to attempt the baddest single stunt currently being performed: the Ghost Ride. Like a hit-and-run in baseball, several factors must combine to make this stunt work. Riding blind, Colbert chases down the riderless bike, allowing just inches between the machines as Daigle remounts. Despite its inherent dangers, given time, somebody is guaranteed to try this one out on the streets.

Cy J. Cyr

Cy J. Cyr

a single discipline. Where the Starboyz favor spontaneous highway antics, LVX, under Pauly Sherer's tutelage, settled on a highly polished routine that is as professional and graceful as a Jackie Chan fight scene. Like Team X-Treem, the Las Vegas Extremes' team features a changing roster of new riders, all of who bring new ideas and talents to the table. Sherer's team took home first-place honors at the first XSBA competition, and, never one to rest on his laurels, he's threatened to produce the world's first X-rated stunt video.

Videos: *Las Vegas Extremes, Las Vegas Extremes 2, Urban Assault, Road Rage, Vegas Knights, Adrenaline*

Like Team X-Treem, the Las Vegas Extremes team features a changing roster of new riders, all of whom bring new ideas and talents to the table.

Cy J. Cyr

Left: A firefighter during the week, Derrick "D-Mann" Daigle, formerly of Las Vegas Extremes, is one of street extreme's most well-known faces.

RIDER: PAULY SHERER

Bike: *Suzuki GSX-R750* Frame protectors, Airtech racing bodywork, Dynojet carbs, steering damper, Yoshimura exhaust.

Favorite Stunt: "My favorite stunt is either the hardest stunt you've ever done or the one you haven't tried yet. A lot of stunts, anybody can do with enough practice, but there are some others—like the Skitch Insane, where you flip from side to side off the bike and slide on your feet—that take forever to learn. I was one of the first riders to do the Flamingo Wheelie, where you hold a stand-up but shoot one foot out behind, and I was doing the See-Saw, where you go from wheelie to stoppie again and again, before anybody else. There aren't many people who can do the Leap of Faith, another move I originated. Somebody once asked what was the first thing they needed to do to learn how to ride stunts and I say, 'It all starts with about four months of ball growing.'"

"My favorite stunt is either the hardest stunt you've ever done or the one you haven't tried yet."—Pauly Sherer, Las Vegas Extremes

Power wheelies made simple by Derrick "D-Mann" Daigle. "You can pop the clutch and get it up, but that makes it easier to flip the bike if you don't know what you're doing. The only way to get comfortable doing this kind of stuff is to practice it all the time."

Index

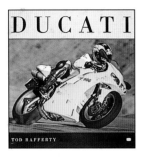
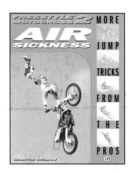
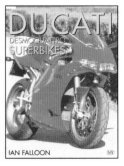

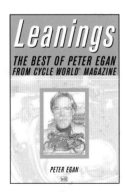
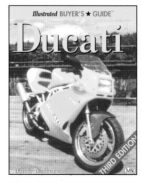
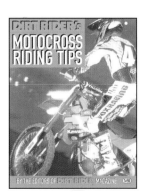